NEW YORK CITY

YESTERDAY & TODAY ™

Linda Tagliaferro

WEST
SIDE
PUBLISHING

Linda Tagliaferro is a native New Yorker and has been a freelance writer for nearly two decades. She was a frequent contributor to *The New York Times* for nine years. Her 39 books for adults, teenagers, and children include *Destination New York, The Complete Idiot's Guide to Decoding Your Genes,* and an A&E Biography book about martial arts legend Bruce Lee. Tagliaferro was born in Brooklyn but has also lived in Manhattan and Staten Island. She currently resides in Queens.

Facts verified by **Adam Michalski.**

Pictured on front cover: Brooklyn Bridge

Yesterday & Today is a trademark of Publications International, Ltd.

West Side Publishing is a division of Publications International, Ltd.

ISBN-13: 978-1-4127-4294-8
ISBN-10: 1-4127-4294-3

Manufactured in China.

8 7 6 5 4 3 2 1

Library of Congress Control Number: 2009924977

At the heart of Central Park, the *Angel of Waters* sculpture stands atop Bethesda Fountain. This neoclassical work of art was unveiled in 1873.

CONTENTS

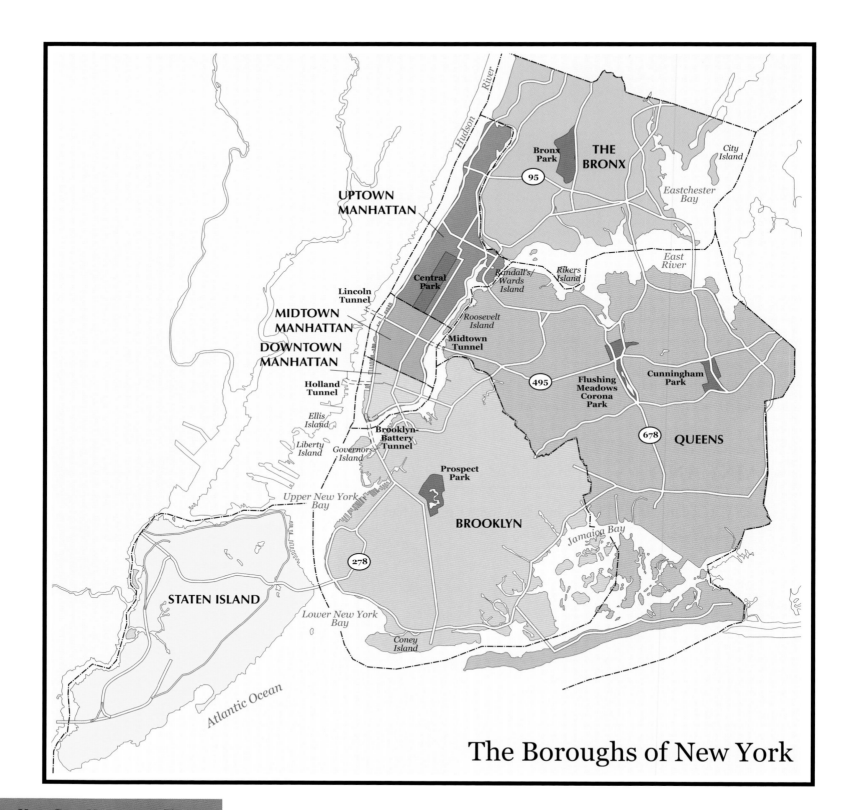

UPTOWN
MANHATTAN

MIDTOWN
MANHATTAN

DOWNTOWN
MANHATTAN

Lincoln
Tunnel

Holland
Tunnel

Central
Park

Midtown
Tunnel

Brooklyn-
Battery
Tunnel

Ellis
Island

Liberty
Island

Governors
Island

Prospect
Park

BROOKLYN

STATEN ISLAND

Upper New York
Bay

Lower New York
Bay

Coney
Island

Atlantic Ocean

Hudson River

Bronx
Park

THE
BRONX

City
Island

Eastchester
Bay

East
River

Randall's
Wards
Island

Rikers
Island

Roosevelt
Island

Flushing
Meadows
Corona
Park

Cunningham
Park

QUEENS

Jamaica Bay

95

495

678

278

The Boroughs of New York

THE PERFECT HARBOR

Since its inception, New York City's destiny has been shaped by its perfect location. Blessed with a deep harbor that is naturally sheltered from storms, the area has always been an ideal place for people to live and trade. Although the goods and services have certainly changed throughout the centuries, New York City, the largest U.S. city by population, has always been about commerce and finance—whether it be the pelts and pottery of yore or today's stocks and Saks Fifth Avenue.

Explorers such as Giovanni da Verrazano and later, Henry Hudson discovered this extraordinary port while the Lenape (one of the original Algonquin-speaking peoples) lived in the area, feasting on the bounty of the harbor's surrounding waters and the flourishing animal populations that once abounded on what is now Manhattan Island.

Trade got its start in the 1600s, as Native Americans offered ample amounts of beaver, mink, and otter pelts to European adventurers in exchange for objects that must have seemed exotic to the native peoples at that time: glass beads, well-fashioned weapons, and other manufactured goods from Europe.

By 1626, the Dutch West India Company established New Amsterdam, a permanent settlement at the very tip of Manhattan's southern shores, surrounded on three sides by water, and later, protected by a high wooden wall. As they did in their homeland, the Dutch built a canal down the middle of their settlement to transport goods in small boats throughout the city.

At this time, the infamous Dutch "purchase" of Manhattan Island occurred. However, while the Dutch thought they were buying the island for 60 guilders (approximately $24), their partners in trade may not have fully understood their intentions—the Lenape had deep respect for the land, and the concept of private ownership was foreign to them.

FROM NEW AMSTERDAM TO NEW YORK

In 1664, the British sailed four imposing warships carrying thousands of soldiers to the colony and, without a fight, took over New Amsterdam. The colony was

As shown in this illustration, Lenape longhouses existed on Manhattan Island before the arrival of the Dutch.

This panoramic photo from 1911 shows City Hall Park in Manhattan.

renamed New York in honor of the Duke of York, the younger brother of King Charles II. The great port thrived under British rule, but when the American Revolution broke out in 1775, the British occupied the city, and devastating fires came close to destroying New York.

REBUILDING TRADE

After the war ended in 1783, New York City rose from the ashes and rebuilt itself and the trade that was an integral part of its identity. New York was the nation's first capital from 1785 to 1790, when it became the largest city in the United States. Trade flourished with the advent of speedy clipper ships and packet ships—the first transatlantic vessels with regularly scheduled sailings.

When the Erie Canal, built by then-mayor DeWitt Clinton, opened on November 4, 1825, the city's connection with Upstate New York brought even

more prestige to the port. Dominating trade with the entire American Midwest via the canal's connection to New York State, the coastal trade with the South, and transatlantic trade with Europe firmly established New York City as the greatest port in the nation.

A CITY OF IMMIGRANTS

During the 19th century, the city became a center of manufacturing; to fill the need for labor, tens of thousands of immigrants, particularly from Ireland and Germany, sailed in steerage to the shores of New York harbor. Along with the thriving industries came the city's first slums, where poorly paid workers lived with their families in Lower East Side tenement apartments. As a result, the more well-to-do, middle-class residents, horrified at the squalor of these buildings, moved to other areas such as Brooklyn Heights, across the East River.

COMMUTING TO WORK

As horse-drawn carriages gave way to streetcars and subways, the era of the commuter emerged. Workers could live in outlying, less-expensive areas that allowed them to escape the decrepit conditions of tenement apartments and still have a convenient way to arrive at work.

Over time, bridges, subways, and tunnels were built that linked far-flung parts of the city. In 1898, the five boroughs—Manhattan, Brooklyn, Queens, the Bronx, and Staten Island—joined to become Greater New York. Soon the city was well on its way to becoming what some people call "The Capital of the World"—a major center of advertising, publishing, broadcasting, entertainment, and more, brimming with magnificent arts institutions, spectacular shopping, fine dining establishments, and musical venues for anything from classical to cool jazz.

In the 20th century, NYC literally and vertically grew with the advent of skyscrapers such as the Woolworth Building and the Empire State Building. New neighborhoods continued to spring up and expand, including SoHo, which started as an industrial area, later turned into a community for artists, and finally became a trendy shopping center and hub of art galleries.

NYC REBUILDS

The most devastating blow to New York City came on September 11, 2001, when terrorists attacked and destroyed the World Trade Center's Twin Towers, killing nearly 3,000 people. But as in the past, New Yorkers showed their resilience in the face of tragedy. In the days following the attack, residents walking down Manhattan's streets or riding the subways seemed to show a strong, silent solidarity.

Like the older city that rose from the ashes of the fires of the American Revolution, modern New York City endures. And when the future One World Trade Center is built on the site of the destroyed World Trade Center, it will point the way to healing in this harbor city that is an unparalleled place of trade, culture, finance, and the indomitable spirit of New Yorkers.

Bright lights, big city: The glitz and glamour of Broadway light up the night.

Lower Manhattan
THE WALLED CITY

Today's Lower Manhattan is the bustling heartbeat of finance and home to various neighborhoods including SoHo and TriBeCa. It includes ethnic areas such as Little Italy and Chinatown, as well as the Lower East Side, which was a garment district where late-18th century immigrants vended their wares as they wheeled their pushcarts from door to door. The Bowery, once a quiet lane leading to the farm owned by New Amsterdam governor Peter Stuyvesant, later became known for its "Bowery bums" and flophouses. Now it has been reborn as the home of multiple art galleries, restaurants, hotels, and an art museum.

However, when the southern tip of Manhattan became home to the Dutch settlement of New Amsterdam in the 17th century, the area was completely different. Established around 1626, this tiny town was little more than a group of houses for 30 families, with a fort and vegetable gardens along the East River. While present-day Manhattan boasts soaring skyscrapers, in the 1660s, the tallest building in New Amsterdam was a mere two-story, whirring windmill. After Trinity Church was completed in 1846, its distinctive spire became the tallest point in this still modestly sized community.

Although the British took control of New Amsterdam in 1664—renaming it New York—the Dutch left a definitive mark on Manhattan; today, some of the rambling patchwork of streets in Lower Manhattan still bear names from the city's Dutch past. Maiden Lane, for example, is a translation of the Dutch name for the street, Maagde Paatje, the former site of a stream where the city's women gathered to wash clothes. In one location where two Dutch-built canals met, New Amsterdam residents hunted beavers. Although the canals were later filled in, the street is still called Beaver Street.

By the middle of the 17th century, residents of New Amsterdam had been concerned that they might be attacked by nearby British colonies, so they erected a

Immigrants arriving at Ellis Island, such as these people in 1920, were subjected to numerous physical and written tests. Some of these examinations were of dubious value, testing for everything from obvious physical ailments to perceived mental disabilities. Medical examiners would then write their assessment on the person's shoulder in chalk— Pg for pregnant or K for a hernia, for example.

Opposite: The old Fulton Fish Market, originally located on the East River waterfront, as it looked in 1943.

The magnificent murals adorning the rotunda of the old New York City Custom House (now the George Gustav Heye Center of the National Museum of the American Indian, seen here in the mid-20th century) were painted by Reginald Marsh. He was paid only 90 cents an hour for his work on the rotunda.

In 1822, an epidemic of yellow fever broke out in a small area of Manhattan; many residents moved up to the cleaner countryside of Greenwich Village to escape the disease.

THE BOHEMIAN SCENE

Starting in the early 1900s, historic Greenwich Village was best known as a haven for artists, intellectuals, and literary figures. Mark Twain, Edna St. Vincent Millay, Herman Melville, and Henry James all called the Village home at one time or another. Famed Welsh poet Dylan Thomas frequented the White Horse Tavern, which opened in 1880. The famous pub is still standing on Hudson Street and West 11th Street. The Village also oversaw the birth of the Beat scene, and artistic luminaries such as Mark Rothko, Jackson Pollock, Norman Rockwell, and Willem de Kooning lived in the Village's bohemian atmosphere.

THE FIRST CAPITAL

Lower Manhattan brims with historic significance. It was the first capital of the United States, and George Washington was sworn in as the nation's first president in Federal Hall. It was in the legendary Fraunces Tavern that he said farewell to his officers at the end of the Revolutionary War in 1783. Both buildings still stand and are popular tourist attractions.

Nowadays, the southern tip of Manhattan is best known for its world-famous Financial District. The name "Wall Street" is synonymous with big business, and the area is home to the New York

tall, wooden wall at the site of the northernmost boundary of their settlement to keep out any possible invaders. In 1699, to make way for the area's continued expansion, the wall came down, but the area where it once stood is now known as Wall Street.

GREENWICH VILLAGE

The area north of New Amsterdam that was considered bucolic countryside in the 1600s later became famous in its own right. The area was already known by the Native Americans as Sapokanican ("tobacco field"), for the land was good for growing tobacco. In the 1630s,

the Dutch claimed the land as their own, and they named this new settlement Noortwyck, or "North District."

When the British took control of New Amsterdam, they also renamed the village of Noortwyck after Greenwich, England. Affluent residents moved to Greenwich Village and erected fashionable estates, including one built in the mid-1700s by Captain Peter Warren, an Irishman who rose in status from a sailor to a British admiral. Other affluent residents followed in his footsteps, including American politicians Alexander Hamilton and Aaron Burr.

Stock Exchange, which traces its roots back to the late 18th century. In 1792, 24 well-respected merchants and stock-brokers met on Wall Street under the shade of a buttonwood tree (also known as the American sycamore). They signed what became known as the Buttonwood Agreement, which outlined their decision to trade securities on a commission basis.

The Financial District was also home to the World Trade Center, which tragically was the site of an Al-Qaeda terrorist attack on September 11, 2001. The attack destroyed the iconic Twin Towers and was responsible for the deaths of almost 3,000 people. Currently, the Tribute WTC Visitor Center serves as a site for visitors to take tours and view exhibits about the people and places that were part of the World Trade Center.

A new World Trade Center has been planned on the original site, but it is not expected to be finished until at least 2013. In the meantime, the Port Authority of New York and New Jersey has plans for its One World Trade Center, which will stand 1,776 feet tall when completed. The building will showcase a proposed 2.6 million square feet of office space, and it will include safety features such as state-of-the-art fireproofing and chemical and biological filters in the air supply system to help prevent future attacks.

The contemporary façade of the New York Stock Exchange is often decorated with American flags.

Left: The Ellis Island Immigration Museum opened on September 10, 1990, after the building had been abandoned for 30 years. Today, more than 40 percent of all Americans have relatives who first came to the United States by passing through Ellis Island.
Above: On posters such as this one from 1935, NYC appeared a glamorous destination.

THE ELLIS ISLAND IMMIGRATION MUSEUM AND THE STATUE OF LIBERTY NATIONAL MONUMENT

Known by a variety of names—including Oyster Island for its plentiful shellfish—Ellis Island had multiple identities as a harbor fort, a gallows site for pirates, and an ammunition depot before President Benjamin Harrison chose it as a gateway for immigrants to the United States.

From 1892 to 1954, Ellis Island in New York Harbor served as the entry point to the United States for more than 12 million immigrants. Steamship passengers braved the two-week journey across the Atlantic in steerage. Once they arrived, they then had to pass inspection before being allowed to start their new lives in the United States. Today, the site houses the Ellis Island Immigration Museum, restored and opened in 1990. Exhibits chronicle the many who passed through the station's Great Hall.

Ellis Island is now part of the Statue of Liberty National Monument and is run by the U.S. National Park Service. Immigrants arriving in the harbor would catch a glimpse of the famed Lady Liberty before disembarking at Ellis Island. A gift from France, the statue was designed by sculptor Frederic Auguste Bartholdi; Alexandre Gustave Eiffel (designer of the Eiffel Tower) masterminded the statue's massive skeletal framework.

Lady Liberty arrived in hundreds of small pieces and was reassembled in New York. On October 28, 1886, thousands of people attended the dedication ceremonies for Liberty Enlightening the World. Standing 111 feet 6 inches, the stately lady was restored in 1986, and her new torch was gilded with 24-karat gold. The seven rays adorning her crown, incidentally, symbolize the seven continents.

Above: Frederic Auguste Bartholdi, dwarfed by his creation, explains to a bystander in 1886 the inner construction of the Statue of Liberty's immense left hand. *Right:* Bartholdi is said to have modeled the face of the Statue of Liberty after his mother's features.

GOVERNORS ISLAND

Just a seven-minute, free ferry ride from Manhattan's Battery Maritime Building, Governors Island seems miles away in spirit. Resembling an idyllic oceanfront hideaway in the country, the island is shaped a bit like an ice cream cone. A large part of the island (92 acres, in fact) has been designated as a National Historic Landmark. The National Park Service also owns and operates land that includes Governors Island National Monument, including historic Castle Williams and Fort Jay, a fortification completed in 1811.

The island initially attracted the local Lenape peoples who fished the bountiful waters off its coast. Centuries later, the British gained ownership of this area, and their governor, Lord Cornbury, built himself a permanent home here. Featuring a church, a historic governor's house, rows of army houses, and more, the island attracts visitors who quietly stroll along the coastline or rent bicycles to ride over one mile of car-free paths that have unobstructed views of New York Harbor and the Statue of Liberty.

Reopening the Island

The Lenape called this island Pagganck, meaning "Nut Island," because the land held many chestnut and hickory trees. It changed hands several times over the years. Above, visitors gather for the first public tour of Governors Island in 200 years, on July 24, 2003.

Only 800 yards from Lower Manhattan, Governors Island was once a strategic fort in New York Harbor, as shown in this 1865 illustration.

THE GEORGE GUSTAV HEYE CENTER OF THE NATIONAL MUSEUM OF THE AMERICAN INDIAN

Before the U.S. government raised money by imposing income taxes in 1916, customs duties were its main source of revenues. The thriving port of New York had its first Custom House located in what is now the Federal Hall National Memorial. By the early 1890s, it was apparent the location was no longer adequate.

At the turn of the century, Cass Gilbert (later the architect of the Woolworth Building) designed a new Custom House. In 1907, the massive Beaux Arts–style building opened as the Alexander Hamilton U.S. Custom House at Bowling Green, near the southern tip of Manhattan. The facility covers three blocks; its ornate façade features monumental sculptures chiseled by Daniel Chester French, whose famous sculpture of Abraham Lincoln sits in the Lincoln Memorial. The building functioned as a customs house until the Customs Service moved its operations in 1973.

In 1994, the George Gustav Heye (pronounced "high") Center opened on the first three floors as one of three such facilities comprising the Smithsonian Institution's National Museum of the American Indian. The museum was named for Heye, a New Yorker who amassed most of the extensive collection, buying directly from Native Americans around the country.

The collection represents a wide range of Native American artisans and includes objects ranging from painted pottery and intricately woven baskets to detailed wooden masks and quilled animal hides. Scheduled museum events include performances of traditional Native American music and dance.

Left: The U.S. Custom House (shown here in 1908), which now houses the George Gustav Heye Center of the National Museum of the American Indian, abounds in decorative sculpture. Crowning the structure is the shield of the United States, which signifies that the building is a Federal structure, not a municipal one. *Below:* A gallery in the National Museum of the American Indian.

U.S. CUSTOM HOUSE N.Y. C.6572
Copyright 1908 by
IRVING UNDERHILL, NEW YORK

WALL STREET AND THE NEW YORK STOCK EXCHANGE

In the 17th century, when New York City was still known as New Amsterdam, residents were wary of the British colonists in other settlements in the New World. In their paranoia, they erected a protective, 12-foot-high wooden stockade at the city's northern boundary. In 1699, after the British took control of the city, the wall came down. The stockade may no longer exist, but the old structure's memory lives on in the name of its former path: Wall Street.

During the 19th century, New York's port was the greatest in the nation, and Wall Street was the center of all the banks, insurance companies, and exchanges that were at the heart of the burgeoning trade. When the city expanded, residents moved northward, but Wall Street's commerce stayed behind and continued to thrive.

The famed New York Stock Exchange (NYSE) grew out of a historic pact made on Wall Street in 1792. There were already various smaller securities markets in Philadelphia, Boston, and New York at the time, but most securities were bought and sold at public auctions by competitive bidding. Twenty-four merchants, hoping to gain control of the securities market, met secretly and planned to set trading fees (to avoid the public auctions) and to trade among themselves.

Since then, the NYSE has become the largest stock exchange in the world. It has been at its current quarters on Wall Street since 1903. In 2007, the NYSE merged with Euronext, bringing together many European and American marketplaces into one global group.

A view of Broad Street south of Wall Street, circa 1916.

Above: A local paper announces the massive decline in stock value on what became known as "Black Thursday," October 24, 1929.
Below: The ornate façade of the Stock Exchange building is crowned by a marble sculpture by John Quincy Adams Ward, titled *Integrity Protecting the Works of Man.*

Above: The floor of the old Stock Exchange at 10 Broad Street in the 1890s, shown in a rare quiet moment.
Right: Traders working on the crowded floor of the modern-day Stock Exchange.

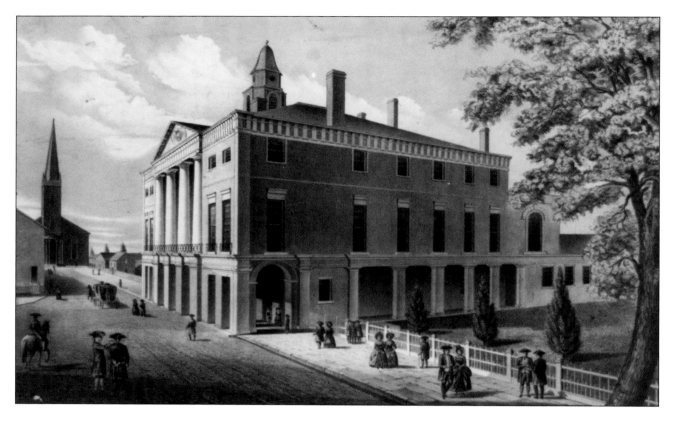

Throughout its three incarnations, Trinity Church, as seen in 1789, has maintained a history of helping the poor. In the early 1700s, the church became the first in the city to minister to African Americans. Notables such as Alexander Hamilton and Robert Fulton were buried in the plot behind the church.

TRINITY CHURCH AND FEDERAL HALL NATIONAL MEMORIAL

In 1698, the steeple of the first Trinity Church dominated the small city's skyline, standing as the first recognizable landmark for ships entering the harbor. Unfortunately, the great New York fire of 1776 left the church in ruins. Part of Trinity Church's parish, St. Paul's Chapel, opened that same year, and it remains the oldest public building in continuous use in Manhattan. A second Trinity Church was built in 1790, but structural defects led to its being demolished in 1839.

The current Trinity Church, designed in the Gothic Revival style, opened in 1846 on Broadway and Wall Street. Trinity's steeple still reaches for the sky, but it is now dwarfed by surrounding skyscrapers. The adjacent Trinity Churchyard is the resting place of many prominent Americans, including Alexander Hamilton and Robert Fulton.

A short walk from the church, Federal Hall National Memorial stands at the site of the original, 18th-century building where George Washington was inaugurated in 1789 as the nation's first president. The first United States Congress also met there, and the Bill of Rights was composed in the original building, which was torn down in 1812.

The present-day Federal Hall National Memorial, which opened in 1842, stands on the original building's site on bustling Wall Street. It served as the site of the Custom House for 20 years, and from 1862 to 1920, it was a U.S. Sub-Treasury building, housing gold bullion in its vaults.

The edifice's steps lead to a statue of the first U.S. president, surrounded by imposing Doric columns reminiscent of the Greek Parthenon. The façade's architectural details were specifically chosen to honor the principles of Greek democracy. Now a museum dedicated to the site's history, it houses exhibits of the significant role Federal Hall played in the founding of the country.

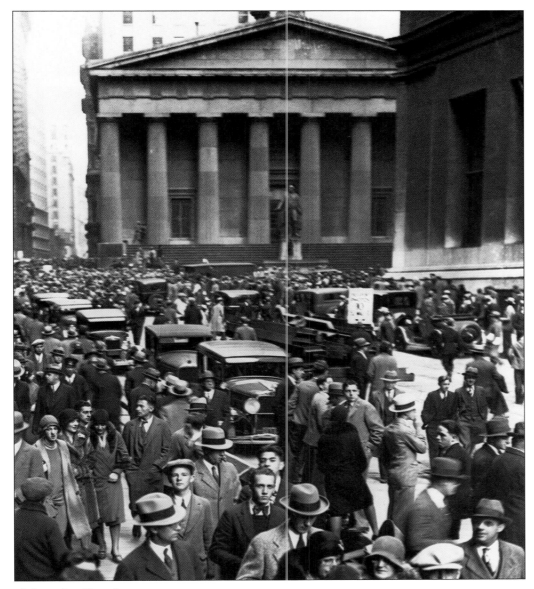

After the Crash

From its earliest days, the building that is now the Federal Hall National Memorial has stood out from its surroundings. Perhaps the building's majestic columns, classical elements, and sturdy design inspired and uplifted these worried people, walking on Wall Street after the 1929 stock market crash.

As tall buildings rose and narrow streets opened up, the steeple of Trinity Church lost its status as the tallest, most recognizable landmark in New York City.

WORLD TRADE CENTER AND GROUND ZERO

In 1959, the Downtown Lower Manhattan Association, brain-child of real estate developer David Rockefeller, promoted the idea of a trade and finance center to revitalize the area. In 1966, construction of the World Trade Center began on a 16-acre site. Over one million cubic yards of earth were excavated, and 10,000 workers erected the building complex that featured the Twin Towers as the centerpiece.

When the towers opened in 1970, they were the world's tallest structures. Their construction required 200,000 tons of steel, more than 40,000 windows, and 99 elevators for the minutes-long ride to the top of the tall towers. A massive underground shopping mall sat directly below the plaza. The World Trade Center even had its own postal zip code: 10048.

In 1993, terrorists drove an explosive-laden truck into the WTC's public parking garage; the resulting detonation killed six people and injured more than 1,000 others. The explosion blasted a five-story-deep crater beneath the towers. The build-ings sustained damage, but repairs brought them back to their original condition.

The Twin Towers survived one attack, but on September 11, 2001, terrorists crashed airplanes directly into the buildings, destroying both towers and killing nearly 3,000 people. The shocked city and nation mourned the loss of the innocent victims, and plans were made for a memorial and a new World Trade Center on the original site, now called Ground Zero.

On July 4, 2004, the cornerstone was laid for the future One World Trade Center, which will rise a symbolic 1,776 feet on the site of the former WTC, in recognition of the year the country gained independence. Construction began in 2006, but legal and economic issues have slowed the progress of the build-ing. It is now projected to open in 2013.

Above: The original Twin Towers were a monumental landmark in Manhattan. Every New Yorker could tell Uptown from Downtown just by looking in the direction of the towering buildings. *Right:* Newspapers across the country reflected America's horror at the attacks.

RESTORING THE WINTER GARDEN ATRIUM

THE OPULENT CENTERPIECE of the World Financial Center, the ten-story, 45,000-square-foot Winter Garden Atrium, opened in 1988. It features inlaid marble floors and live palm trees that flourish underneath an arched dome of glass panels within the center. Originally standing across from the World Trade Center, and with a pedestrian bridge that once connected the atrium to the WTC, the building was severely damaged during the terrorist attacks of September 11, 2001.

Extensive repairs were made on the atrium, and on September 17, 2002, the Winter Garden reopened. It continues to host free concerts, food festivals, dance events, and art exhibits.

An architectural drawing of the proposed successor to the fallen World Trade Center. Although the original plans called for the new structure to be called Freedom Tower, the name was changed to One World Trade Center (shown at far left).

Bank workers bundle cash into packages after counting. The packs were then tightly strapped with steel bands to prevent theft, as shown in this photo from the 1920s.

FEDERAL RESERVE BANK

Under British rule, colonists were not allowed to mint their own money. Instead, New York's earliest residents had to barter to obtain the goods and services they needed. When the Revolutionary War broke out, the Continental Congress financed it by borrowing heavily from other nations, including the Netherlands and France. After issuing too much paper money (called "Continentals"), America found itself in the middle of raging inflation, hence the phrase "not worth a Continental."

After several attempts at creating a national bank, and economic crises that occurred in the 18th and 19th centuries, the U.S. government considered major reforms in the banking system. In 1913, Congress created an independent governmental entity to function as the country's central bank. For this reason, the "Fed" has been referred to as "a bank for banks." Among its responsibilities, the Fed formulates and executes monetary policy in the United States, seeking to keep the economy stable and avoid inflation or recession.

Federal Reserve Bank Building, New York.

The Federal Reserve Bank of New York opened in 1924; by 1927, its vaults held an astounding 10 percent of the world's monetary gold.

The Federal Reserve System comprises 12 regional reserve banks across the country and a Board of Governors in Washington, D.C. The Federal Reserve Bank of New York is one of these regional banks. The neo-Renaissance building, completed in 1924, fills an entire block, and it resembles a Florentine palazzo with limestone façade and ornate ironwork.

Sitting on a solid base of the city's bedrock, 50 feet below sea level, the bank's gold vault securely stores billions of dollars' worth of gold bullion, exceeding even Fort Knox's holdings. Separate rooms store money for 60 accounts, some from foreign nations. Although most funds are currently transferred by wire, if a country holding an account wishes to pay another country in gold, then the required number of gold bars are physically moved from one storeroom to another.

The Romanesque Revival–style Federal Reserve building stands tall at Liberty Street in the city's Financial District.

THE SOUTH STREET SEAPORT

For more than 40 years during the 19th century, the heart of New York City's thriving port stood at Fulton and South streets on the East River. Sheltered from the winds and ice that sometimes plagued the Hudson River, this area was once lined with moored ships that traveled to and from all parts of the world. Nearby, sailmakers and figurehead carvers shared the streets with boarding houses and bordellos. But after the 1880s, many sea captains preferred the Hudson River's deeper waters, which could accommodate larger ships, and the area lost its favored port status.

In 1967, the South Street Museum opened, and the area was slowly restored in the late '70s. During the '80s, the area was once again a vibrant district, emphasized by the opening of Pier 17, a large mall with a spectacular view of the Brooklyn Bridge.

Moored at the South Street Seaport is an impressive collection of historic ships such as the four-masted baroque *Peking* (built in 1911) and the *Lettie G. Howard* (built in 1893), one of the oldest surviving fishing schooners in the United States.

The Seaport hosts a number of events throughout the year, including music festivals in the summer and its annual Christmas Tree Lighting celebration. In 2008, the Seaport introduced its 8,000-square-foot ice skating rink, Seaport Ice.

The Seaport has a long-term proposed plan for its future redevelopment, subject to the city's public reviews process. The plan includes nearly tripling the existing Seaport's open areas, building a new community space for performances and lectures, and constructing a new water-taxi slip.

NEW YORK CITY HALL AND THE WOOLWORTH BUILDING

The current New York City Hall, built in 1812, is one of the seats of the city's government as well as the oldest continuously used city hall in the United States. Designed by John McComb Jr. and Francois Mangin, the impressive façade features arched windows and stately columns; under its rotunda, presidents Abraham Lincoln and Ulysses S. Grant were laid in state.

City Hall's prestigious portrait collection represents some of the leading 18th- and 19th-century American artists. A former pasture, the surrounding City Hall Park now serves as an urban oasis for office workers and others. The park's bicycle path leads to the nearby Brooklyn Bridge, where cyclists can pedal across to the neighboring borough.

Across the street from City Hall stands the Woolworth Building, which was the world's tallest building from 1913 until 1930, when its 55 stories were eclipsed by the Chrysler Building and 40 Wall Street. Once referred to as the "Cathedral of Commerce" for its resemblance to a Gothic church, it became the corporate headquarters of F. W. Woolworth's "five-and-dime store" retail empire from its 1913 opening until it was sold in 1998. It was designed by Cass Gilbert, who later designed the U.S. Supreme Court building.

Inside, the lobby brims with marble decoration, a stained glass ceiling, and gargoyle caricatures representing Woolworth, Gilbert, and others.

An aerial view of City Hall Park in 1938. In the background are the Municipal Building, the Pulitzer Building, and the Tribune Building.

Lit From Within

On the night of April 24, 1913, the Woolworth Building's (as seen on the left) opening was celebrated with President Woodrow Wilson pressing a button from within the White House that simultaneously lit up every floor. The architects clearly enjoyed themselves: In the lobby of the Woolworth Building is a whimsical bronze gargoyle caricature of architect Cass Gilbert (inset), holding a mini version of the skyscraper he designed.

FINE DINING COMES TO NEW YORK

GIOVANNI AND PIETRO DEL-MONICO, brothers from a Swiss town, opened a small shop in New York City in 1827. Their wares included savory pastries, fine coffee and wines, mouthwatering chocolates, and Havana cigars. The shop was highly successful, and in 1837, the brothers opened the country's first fine dining establishment. Although New York already had plenty of small cafés and taverns, Delmonico's was the first exclusive establishment of its kind outside of Europe.

The Delmonico's address has changed several times, but the opulent restaurant has been in almost continuous operation since its opening in the 19th century. The current incarnation of the restaurant is at 56 Beaver Street in Lower Manhattan (pictured). Through the years, princes, presidents, and prominent figures such as Mark Twain, Nikola Tesla, Charles Dickens, and Queen Victoria have relished Delmonico's signature steaks and fine wines.

A number of culinary firsts came out of Delmonico's kitchens. Their chefs take credit for creating Lobster Newburg, Baked Alaska (to commemorate the United States purchase of Alaska), and the renowned Delmonico's steak.

SOHO AND TRIBECA

New York City's SoHo district was named for its location: SOuth of HOuston (pronounced "HOW-ston") Street. Originally an industrial area, many of its buildings took advantage of cast-iron architecture, a 19th-century innovation. Instead of paying top dollar for stone columns with chiseled ornaments, builders could incorporate the products of cast-iron foundries, which distributed catalogs of available façades. Although the cast-iron products were hollow inside, the ornate columns and detailed decorations could easily be installed and painted to look like marble.

In the 1960s, artists were drawn to the cheap rents and expansive lofts of the area. Eventually, the area attracted galleries and boutiques for trendy jewelry and clothing. Today, SoHo rents have continued to rise, and the streets are lined with designer stores such as Prada and Coach.

To the south of SoHo lies TriBeCa (short for the "TRIangle BElow CAnal Street"), which is also a former industrial area that experienced a rejuvenation when its textile factories and other spaces were reborn as luxury condominiums and rentals. The area's most famous champion is actor Robert De Niro, who founded the TriBeCa Film Festival in 2002. The annual event features independent documentaries, features, and short films.

Opposite: Constructed in the 1800s, the Haughwout Building (shown here in 1857) at the corner of Broadway and Broome Street featured many modern amenities including the world's first passenger elevator. Today, colorful red and white awnings line the façade of the Staples store housed within.

In SoHo, whimsical colors brighten up typical New York City fire escapes.

Many SoHo buildings have been painted by trompe-l'oeil architectural muralist Richard Haas. Visitors and natives alike enjoy figuring out the 3-D optical illusions.

SoHo is famous for its hip boutiques, such as this row of trendy shops on Wooster Street.

Right: Although Little Italy is decreasing in size, the yearly San Gennaro Festival (shown here in 2004) continues to draw huge crowds with its tempting display of Italian culinary specialties. *Below:* From the early days of Italian immigration (here, circa 1900), street vendors always had plenty of buyers for their wares.

LITTLE ITALY

In the 1800s, tens of thousands of Italians moved to New York seeking a better life, and many of them settled on or near Mulberry Street. Italian shops and restaurants soon filled the neighborhood, and the area became known as Little Italy. As second generation Italians raised in the neighborhood move away, present-day Little Italy is diminishing. Now Chinatown's growth encroaches on the neighborhood, but today's Little Italy still features dozens of Italian restaurants, including Umberto's Clam House, which was the infamous scene of mafioso Joey Gallo's murder in 1972.

Every year, usually around the last two weeks of September, Mulberry Street is closed to traffic from Canal and Bayard streets to make way for the 11-day San Gennaro festival. Started in 1926 by Neapolitan immigrants, the festival features parades and a Grand Procession in honor of the patron saint of Naples. Colorful lights illuminate the streets, where rows of vendors sell Italian specialties such as fried calamari, sizzling sausage, pepper and onion sandwiches, and pastries including cannolis and zeppole.

CHINATOWN

South of Little Italy, Chinatown got its start in the 1800s, when Chinese immigrants flocked to the areas near Canal Street. Even today, the bustling streets brim with shops, food vendors, and restaurants featuring a variety of Asian foods, including Chinese, Vietnamese, Malaysian, and Thai cuisines.

At the foot of the Manhattan Bridge is Chinatown's Mahayana Buddhist Temple, a serene space where visitors are welcome to enter. A tall, golden Buddha statue sits on a lotus blossom, while flickering candles provide a dim light and the scent of incense wafts gently throughout.

The annual Chinese New Year celebrates the lunar New Year, and it typically falls between late January and mid-February. Festival highlights include dragon- and lion-dancers, a parade with decorative floats, and colorful fireworks.

Above: By 1909, when this picture was taken, Chinatown was already the growing home to waves of Chinese immigrants.
Left: From its earliest days to the present, colorful Chinatown has always offered unique gifts, culinary delights, and fresh produce, including exotic Asian vegetables.

THE LOWER EAST SIDE AND THE AMATO OPERA

The area bounded by the East Village, Chinatown, and the East River has long been associated with its historic influx of immigrants. The Lower East Side has certainly changed over the years: first as pastoral farmland, then as the infamous home to crowded tenements, and now to its current revival.

Early immigrants included Italian, German, and Polish newcomers to the United States. For years, the Lower East Side was known as a center for those of the Jewish faith, and many historic synagogues still remain. Katz's deli, established in 1888, continues to draw customers with classic pastrami sandwiches slathered in mustard, with a side of sour pickles.

On the Bowery, just west of the Lower East Side, is the Amato Opera. With just over 100 seats, the theater has offered grand opera in an intimate setting since 1964. Originally founded in 1948 by Italian immigrants Anthony and Sally Amato, the first performances were staged in various venues before moving to the Amato's current location.

In 1973, the Amato became the unlikely neighbor to the underground rock venue CBGB, which hosted more than 30 years' worth of music acts, including Pavement, The Jam, and the Ramones. The raucous club closed its doors in 2006.

In December 2007, the Bowery celebrated the opening of the first permanent home of the New Museum of Contemporary Art. The avant-garde building resembles a skewed pile of blocks, adorned by a gleaming aluminum mesh façade.

The Lower East Side is now experiencing rapid gentrification, its seedy past becoming lost in new restaurants and upscale condominiums.

Although the stage at the Amato Opera is small, the performances have always been in colorful, grand style. Here, the cast performs Franz Lehár's classic operetta *The Merry Widow*.

Below: Known as the godfathers of punk rock, the Ramones (performing in 1976) were among the many famed groups who played at the legendary CBGB club.

Fashion designer John Varvatos's boutique now operates in the old CBGB location. Varvatos kept many of the old club's signature elements, including walls full of band stickers and concert flyers.

Right: The façade of the modern-day Eldridge Street Synagogue contains Gothic, Moorish Revival, and Romanesque elements.

Below: The Eldridge Street Synagogue, built in 1887, was a house of worship for many Eastern European Jewish immigrants. Nearly 100 years later, the building was in danger of collapsing. After a 20-year restoration, the synagogue was restored to its former glory and reopened in 2007.

Above: The avant-garde New Museum of Contemporary Art gleams at night. Designed by noted architects Kazuyo Sejima and Ryue Nishizawa of the Tokyo-based partnership SANAA, the museum brings a new vitality to the Bowery.

GREENWICH VILLAGE

Native Americans once called this swampland Sapokanican. During Dutch colonization, this area to the north of New Amsterdam was named Noortwyck, and it was primarily used for growing tobacco. It was the British who gave the area its current name, Greenwich Village.

During the early 1800s, many New Yorkers moved to the area to get away from the epidemics raging elsewhere in the city. The wealthy built estates in the village, while freed slaves worked the land on farms near today's Minetta Lane. In the mid-20th century, beatniks and bohemians frequented the West Village (the area west of 7th Avenue), and the area became the birthplace of the Beat Movement. Residents and out-of-towners alike visited popular places such as the Café Figaro and Trude Heller's.

Once considered a working-class section of the Lower East Side, the East Village came into its own in the '60s when hippies moved in. The Electric Circus pulsed with strobe lights and loud music, and the Fillmore East, dubbed "The Church of Rock and Roll," presented concerts by The Doors and The Who. Both venues closed in 1971.

Today, as with many of New York City's boroughs, both the East and West Villages have been gentrified and real estate prices have skyrocketed. Alongside traditional brownstones with wide stoops, upscale restaurants and swanky shops have sprung up throughout the Village.

Cooper Square

In the early 1900s, Cooper Square (above) was a popular meeting place. In the modern photo, the building with the American flag waving at its top is Cooper Union, a college that trains artists, architects, and engineers. Formally known as Cooper Union for the Advancement of Science and Art, the educational institution was founded by inventor and philanthropist Peter Cooper in 1859.

The East Village was home to hippies in the 1960s. As seen in this modern-day photo, the colorful, eclectic neighborhood still attracts a bohemian crowd, as well as droves of tourists.

Opposite: Formerly used as a parade ground, Washington Square Park was the backdrop for a 1919 WWI victory parade by the paratroopers of the 82nd Airborne Division. The soldiers had victoriously parachuted four times into enemy territory. *Inset:* During the warmer months, Washington Square Park, with its fountain and famous arch, often attracts street performers, chess players, and residents who bring their canine friends to the park's enclosed dog run.

Jefferson Market Library

The Jefferson Market Library building was once a courthouse. Designed by Frederick Clark Withers and Calvert Vaux, the Victorian Gothic building was constructed from 1875–1877, along with an adjoining market and prison. In 1896, Stephen Crane, author of *The Red Badge of Courage*, testified here on behalf of a woman falsely accused of prostitution. In 1906, millionaire Harry K. Thaw was tried here for the murder of famed architect Stanford White. One hundred feet above the street, the building's tower was used to watch for fires. The original bell that alerted volunteer firefighters still hangs in the tower.

THE MEATPACKING DISTRICT AND THE HIGH LINE

In the early 20th century, the area to the far west of the West Village was known only as the home of hundreds of meatpacking plants. By the 1980s, transvestites, drug dealers, and prostitutes frequented the area. In 1985, the Florent restaurant opened in the mostly forgotten area; by the '90s, the Meatpacking District (MPD) had transformed into one of the city's hippest neighborhoods.

Designer boutiques such as Stella McCartney and Diane von Furstenburg are now in the MPD, and art galleries add a cultural flair to the area. Restaurants such as Spice Market and Buddakan serve gourmet meals in exotic settings, and local clubs entertain late-night revelers. In 2004, the upscale Hotel Gansevoort opened with its rooftop Plunge Bar offering expansive views of the Hudson River.

Above the MPD, the High Line, often called "a park in the sky," opened in 2009. The green, 1½-mile space is a reconstruction of an old elevated freight railway from the 1930s that once ran from Midtown to the area. The freight trains had direct links to warehouses, and they could deliver meat, produce, and other goods right into the buildings.

The tracks were abandoned by the '80s, however, and they were soon overgrown with weeds and wildflowers. Hoping to restore the historic structure and transform it into a raised park, a group called the Friends of the High Line formed in 1999, and they started a grassroots campaign to save the elevated rail structure and transform it into a tranquil green space open to the public.

At the time when this photo was taken in 1911, so many pedestrians were accidentally killed by railcars at West 26th Street and Eleventh Avenue that it became known as "Death Avenue."

Above: Once an overgrown, elevated section of the Meatpacking District (as shown here), the High Line's revitalization includes plans for walkways and gardens. The project's landscape architeture is designed by Field Operations, and its architecture is designed by Diller Scofidio + Renfro. *Right:* Housed in an old 9th Avenue Nabisco cookie factory, Buddakan is a restaurant high on theatrical glamour.

Vento Trattoria shines at night on Hudson Street and 14th. The restaurant's lounge includes alcoves that were formerly part of the original building's horse stables.

NOTABLE NEW YORKERS

From its earliest days, "The City That Never Sleeps" has been a home for both the famous and the infamous. From the first Native American inhabitants to the Dutch and British colonists and the waves of immigration that followed, NYC has sheltered millions of people, all with their own unique stories.

Poets and politicians, authors and athletes—all types of people thrive in New York City, regardless of occupation, color, or creed. Basketball star Kareem Abdul-Jabbar was born in the Inwood section of Upper Manhattan, while comedian Whoopi Goldberg was raised in Chelsea. Singer/actress Jennifer Lopez proudly touts her upbringing in a Latino neighborhood in the South Bronx, and salsa king Tito Puente lived in Spanish Harlem.

But you don't have to be born in New York to become a New Yorker. The city's reputation as a mecca of art, music, business, and theater has long lured people from near and far to become long-time residents. Former Beatle John Lennon moved to NYC from England. Along with his Japanese wife, Yoko Ono, the couple lived in Manhattan for many years.

Brooklyn-born opera star Beverly Sills, world-famous diva Maria Callas, gangster Al Capone, writer and director Woody Allen, Supreme Court judge Ruth Bader Ginsburg—the five boroughs have produced a vast array of New York notables; it would take a separate book just to list them all. Instead, here is just a small sampling of the many proud sons and daughters of the Big Apple.

Acclaimed architect and landscape designer Frederick Law Olmsted (seen here in 1893) was born in Hartford, Connecticut. At age 18, he moved to New York City and initially set up a farm in Staten Island. He eventually turned to landscape design, and he teamed up with Calvert Vaux to design Central Park and Prospect Park.

London-born Calvert Vaux, master architect and landscape designer, spent 40 years of his life in New York City. Although he is best known for his collaborations with Olmsted on Central Park and Prospect Park, Vaux also contributed to designs for the White House grounds and Smithsonian Institute. He is pictured here in the late 1800s.

Emma Lazarus, shown here in the late 1800s, was born to Sephardic Jewish parents in New York City. She is best remembered for her poem "The New Colossus," which reads, "Give me your tired, your poor, your huddled masses yearning to breathe free." Her words now grace the pedestal of the Statue of Liberty.

Lena Horne dazzles in 1947. The sultry African American songstress and actress was born in the Bedford-Stuyvesant area of Brooklyn. She won numerous Grammy awards, including one in 1962 for Best Female Vocal Performance in *Porgy and Bess.*

Mayor Fiorella H. LaGuardia waves goodbye on his last day in office in 1946. LaGuardia was also affectionately known as "The Little Flower," a direct translation of his first name from Italian. He was born in Greenwich Village to Italian immigrant parents and was a graduate of N.Y.U. One of his early jobs was as an interpreter at Ellis Island; there he saw first-hand how some families were broken up when officials refused to let some immigrants into the United States. The much-loved politician served as mayor of NYC for three terms.

Actor Robert De Niro (seen here in 1995) grew up in Manhattan's Little Italy neighborhood. In 1974, he won an Academy Award for Best Supporting Actor for his role in *The Godfather: Part II,* and in 1980, he won an Oscar for Best Actor in *Raging Bull.* He revitalized the TriBeCa area of NYC when he instituted the TriBeCa Film Festival. He also has part ownership in the TriBeCa Grill restaurant.

The daughter of Chinese immigrants, fashion designer Vera Wang was raised on the Upper East Side. She is known primarily for her bridal apparel: Celebrities including Jennifer Lopez, Uma Thurman, and Victoria Beckham have donned her upscale wedding gowns.

A former four-star general, Colin Powell was born in Harlem to Jamaican immigrants and raised in the South Bronx. Later in life, Powell served under former President Ronald Reagan. Under former President George W. Bush, Powell became the first African American to serve as U.S. Secretary of State, as seen here in 2002.

Midtown Manhattan

FROM COUNTRYSIDE TO METROPOLIS

Resting roughly between 14th Street and 59th Street, today's Midtown is the vibrant heart of Manhattan. The sights and sounds of Midtown are what most tourists envision when making their plans to visit New York City.

Once a tranquil countryside, this section of Manhattan was forever changed by the advent of new forms of transportation such as the el, or elevated trains, that expanded throughout Manhattan, and eventually into most of the Outer Boroughs. Up to this point, Wall Street had been the heart of the city, but the trains made other areas of the city more accessible. This and other elements led to New York's midtown expansion.

New York began to grow up as well as out. Elisha Otis's invention of the elevator in the mid-1800s freed architects from designing buildings that were only a few stories tall. In addition, new steel construction methods allowed buildings to soar ever higher, leading to the skyscrapers that make up the vertical city that is present-day New York.

The Fuller Building—later called the Flatiron Building for its unique shape, which resembles a certain appliance used for pressing clothes—rose 21 stories high, and was one of the tallest buildings in New York when it was built in 1903. The structure still stands where Broadway, 5th Avenue, and 23rd Street converge. It also lent its name to the surrounding area, now known as the Flatiron District. Towering structures such as the Art Deco–inspired Chrysler Building and the Empire State Building followed.

In the 1870s, wealthy New Yorkers lived in style around fashionable areas such as Union Square, Madison Square, and Gramercy Square. Some of these sections of the city even boasted their own gated and locked parks, set aside specifically for the pleasure of local residents.

Opposite: Years before its tragic sinking from a German U-boat attack in 1915, the British luxury ocean liner *Lusitania* completed its maiden voyage by arriving at Chelsea Piers on September 13, 1907.
Right: Light streams into a quiet Pennsylvania Station in 1911.

Untold numbers of people have used the four-faced brass clock as a meeting point in Grand Central Terminal's main concourse. Each clock face is made of opal, and the clock's worth is estimated between $10 million and $20 million. During the building's renovation in the late 1990s, the clock was moved just slightly to align with the building's compass points.

But not every part of the island was reserved for the rich. Slums also began to develop around the island. During this time, New York's Tenderloin district sprang up between the former slums in Hell's Kitchen and the refined areas of Fifth Avenue. An el train ran along 6th Avenue, and eateries and dance halls came to the district. Brothels sprang up as well, taking advantage of the increased traffic in the area.

SHOP 'TIL YOU DROP

In 1862, Irish entrepreneur A. T. Stewart relocated his large retail store from Broadway and Chambers Street to a palatial setting with a sumptuous cast-iron façade on 9th Street and Broadway. This inspired others to open their own stores nearby, and eventually an increasingly well-known shopping area developed. Dubbed the Ladies' Mile, it stretched from 9th Street to 23rd Street between Broadway and 6th Avenue, and it lured the most fashion-conscious women of the time, including the wives of presidents Cleveland and Grant, to the numerous elegant shops.

Not long after, Benjamin Altman opened a store on 18th Street; others soon followed. Lord & Taylor opened on Broadway and 20th Street. In 1896, the Siegel-Cooper Dry Goods Store, located on 18th Street and 6th Avenue, was the largest department store in the world. The steel-frame structure was lavishly covered in real marble, copper, and bronze. The six-story building extended across an entire block, and riders on the el train could catch a glimpse of the rich décor inside on the building's second floor. (It is now occupied by Bed Bath & Beyond.)

BY THE BRIDGE

The Brooklyn Bridge opened in 1883, providing a quick, convenient link between Manhattan and what was then the city of Brooklyn. Soon, the bridge—and the connection it provided—gave rise to the creation of new neighborhoods throughout Manhattan. These included Chelsea and Murray Hill, suburban areas featuring row after row of houses. The New York City landscape was changing, and the surrounding areas changed with it as suburbia slowly displaced the farmland that had once been the region's dominant feature.

MODERN MIDTOWN

Now home to the nation's largest central business district, Midtown is the destination of many who live in the Outer Boroughs, who commute to their jobs in this concentrated area. In addition to its numerous office buildings, Midtown also encompasses the world-famous neon glitz found in Times Square and the Theater District, where Broadway shows entertain thousands of people nightly.

Midtown also features impressive train stations such as Grand Central Terminal (also known as Grand Central Station) and Pennsylvania Station (simply known as Penn Station), both of which serve as the focal points for employees and other visitors coming in from Long Island, various boroughs, and points north and south of the city.

Fifth Avenue, once home to legendary mansions owned by the wealthiest New Yorkers, is now known for its variety of shops that offer "retail therapy" to shopaholics, including the Apple Store, open 24 hours a day for fans of computers and iPods, and decidedly upscale stores such as Tiffany & Company, Louis Vuitton, and Prada.

Midtown Manhattan is divided into a number of smaller neighborhoods, each with its own distinct character. Hell's Kitchen, which stretches from 8th Avenue to the Hudson River, between 34th Street and 42nd Street, was once a seamy area that only the bravest souls dared walk through. But with the development that crept into all parts of the city, Hell's Kitchen is now home to restaurants and condominiums.

Further east, Koreatown features a small strip of restaurants and shops on 32nd Street. The ethnic enclave developed in the 1980s, and today it offers Korean food such as homemade kimchi and dumplings, plus a number of karaoke establishments where you can rent a room to show off your singing skills in private—without standing in front of a crowd of strangers. There's even a vegetarian Korean restaurant, Hangawi, built to resemble a serene Korean Buddhist monastery, where low tables and dim lighting add a tranquil note to savory meals.

Worshippers attend service at Saint Patrick's Cathedral in Midtown Manhattan. The cathedral can seat approximately 2,200 people.

UNION SQUARE

Although Union Square was historically the scene of many workers' protests and political rallies, it wasn't named for labor unions. The area, formerly part of a farm, received its name in the 1800s for its location at the "union" of the former Bloomingdale Road (now Broadway) and Bowery Road (now 4th Avenue.)

In 1839, following the lead of the designers of London's fashionable squares, Union Square opened as a park, with a fountain at its center. During this time, theaters, concert halls, and aristocratic residences surrounded the area.

More than 30 years later, renowned landscape architects Frederick Law Olmsted and Calvert Vaux redesigned the park. Verdant trees and shrubs lined the paths, and statues were placed at various points throughout the park.

Union Square has been the scene of a number of historic events. In 1882, it was the backdrop for the nation's first Labor Day celebration, with crowds of thousands of workers parading down Broadway. More than a century later, after the tragic events of September 11, 2001, many people who lost loved ones congregated at the park and set up makeshift memorials with photos of victims of the terrorist attacks. Mourners lit candles and placed flowers among the temporary shrines.

Today, the park offers a tranquil green space at the beginning of Midtown Manhattan. Union Square's Greenmarket provides an open-air venue for shoppers to buy fresh produce from local farms, while the Union Square Holiday Market features stalls with vendors of handmade jewelry, soaps, and organic baked goods.

The U.S.S. *Recruit* was a wooden model of a battleship that stood from 1917 to 1920 in Union Square as a World War I recruiting station. According to a *New York Times* article, the "battleship" was responsible for 25,000 men signing up. The recruiting station was later moved to Luna Park in Coney Island.

Union Square

Union Square's expanse of lush greenery lies between 14th and 17th streets (left). With its entrance to several subways at the 14th Street/Union Square stop, the park bustles with crowds of New Yorkers and tourists. Below, Henry Kirke Brown's bronze equestrian statue of George Washington is the oldest sculpture in New York City's parks, dating from 1856. It originally stood in the middle of the street in an enclosure but was later moved to its present location within Union Square's park.

Left: Since its opening in 1976, the Greenmarket features ripe tomatoes, fresh apples and pears, and more for sale, direct from local farms. Crowds of shoppers are also drawn to the many delights found at the square, such as tempting pumpkin pies, mushroom quiches, and gourmet brick oven–baked breads.

CHELSEA

Today's Chelsea neighborhood, running roughly from 15th Street to 29th Street on the West Side, offers a lively nightlife. Currently a center of gay-friendly Manhattan, Chelsea was once serene farmland. In 1750, sea captain Thomas Clarke purchased land and retired here. He reputedly named his estate after London's Chelsea Royal Hospital.

In the late 1800s, Chelsea boasted a Grand Opera House, which became a movie theater in 1960. The present-day neighborhood still features cultural venues such as the Joyce Theater and the People's Improv Theater.

The area's most famous lodging, the Hotel Chelsea, is housed in a building that, from its inception in 1883, was the city's first cooperative apartments. In fact, until 1899 its 12 stories comprised what was then NYC's tallest building.

In 1905, the building was transformed into a hotel. Literary and artistic luminaries lived here for long or short periods, including writers such as Allen Ginsberg, Arthur Miller, and Dylan Thomas, who succumbed to alcohol poisoning in his room. Throughout the years, the hotel's roster has included celebrities such as Thomas Wolfe,

Janis Joplin, and Jimi Hendrix. Perhaps the hotel is most remembered as the site where Sex Pistol Sid Vicious murdered his girlfriend, Nancy Spungen.

In 1912, the ill-fated *Titanic* never arrived at its intended destination, the original Chelsea Piers. In 1915, the *Lusitania* sailed from the Chelsea Piers' docks. Much has changed. Chelsea Piers Sports & Entertainment Complex now spans 30 acres fronting the Hudson River. The building houses, among other venues, an indoor skating rink, a microbrewery, and a multitiered, outdoor golf driving range resembling a beehive.

Left: Billing itself as "a rest stop for rare individuals," the Hotel Chelsea (seen here in the early '50s) lives up to its name. While in residence at the storied building, Arthur C. Clarke penned *2001: A Space Odyssey. Below:* The lobby of the Hotel Chelsea (seen here in 2007) has hosted a wide array of guests, from Mark Twain to Tennessee Williams, Stanley Kubrick to Dee Dee Ramone.

Above: The Chelsea Piers Golf Range (right), as seen from the Hudson River in 2005.
Inset: Chelsea Piers is home to the only golf driving range in Manhattan. Golfers face the Hudson River as they practice their swings from the four-tiered structure. Although it looks as if the golfers are aiming for the nearby river, sturdy nets prevent the golf balls from winding up in the water.

'ROUND THE WORLD WITH NELLIE BLY

Born Elizabeth Jane Cochran in 1864, the investigative journalist who became known as Nellie Bly was best known for her exposé of the New York Lunatic Asylum on Blackwell's Island (now called Roosevelt Island.) After writing about her terrifying ten-day stay at the mental institution, she went on to tour the world in 1889. Reporting for *The New York World,* she also set out to break the fictitious record set by the character Phileas Fogg in Jules Verne's novel *Around the World in Eighty Days.*

On November 14, 1889, armed with just one small piece of luggage, Bly boarded the Hamburg-American Company's ship the *Augusta Victoria* at the pier in Hoboken, New Jersey. As she voyaged to places such as London; Ismaïlia, Egypt; Singapore; and Hong Kong, the daring young reporter wrote daily of her experiences. The *World*'s readers eagerly followed her exploits as she traveled by ship, train, horse, burro, and rickshaw.

Exactly 72 days, 6 hours, 11 minutes, and 14 seconds after boarding the *Augusta Victoria,* Bly arrived back in the United States, breaking the "record" of 80 days. Considering the limited modes of transportation available in the 19th century, this was hailed as an amazing feat. Regaled with parades and fireworks in her honor, songs written about her, and even a board game, called 'Round the World with Nellie Bly, the plucky reporter had come home to worldwide fame.

GRAMERCY PARK AND MADISON SQUARE PARK

When Native Americans lived in the area now called Gramercy Park, they frequented the small brook that started here. Abounding in trout, the water flowed all the way down to what is now Minetta Lane in the West Village before finally emptying into the Hudson near today's West Houston Street. Today, the area is home to upscale condos and an exclusive park. Only residents and guests of the nearby Gramercy Park Hotel are permitted to enter the gated park.

The Gramercy Park neighborhood (roughly 17th Street to 22nd Street, between Park Avenue South and 2nd Avenue) has long been a prestigious address. In the mid-19th century, mansions and brownstones filled the streets surrounding the small park. In 1864, Pete's Tavern was built on 18th Street and Irving Place, and it still remains NYC's oldest continuously operating bar and restaurant. Writer O. Henry frequented the watering hole and composed his famous short story *The Gift of the Magi* here in his favorite booth in 1904.

Nearby Madison Square Park was named for the fourth U.S. president, James Madison, known as "the father of the Constitution." In the late 1700s, the area had been used as a potter's field, a place to bury the poor and unidentified dead. Later the burial ground was moved to present-day Washington Square Park in the West Village. By 1806, the land was home to a U.S. Army Arsenal; later it was made the scene of festive military parades. From 1825 until 1839, the Arsenal acted as a "House of Refuge" for troubled teenagers, until the building burned to the ground.

Eventually, the land was used primarily for recreation; in fact, some sports historians maintain that the park saw the birth of baseball, since Alexander Cartwright formed his first baseball club there in 1845. Only two years later, Madison Square Park formally opened to the public. The first Madison Square Garden, built in 1879, was named for the area and was adjacent to the park.

Today, office buildings and retail shops surround Madison Square Park. The tranquil green space serves as a backdrop for several public programs, including Madison Square Music's free, live concerts and Madison Square Art's outdoor exhibitions.

Hotel Gramercy Park
East 21st Street
New York

Above: Founded in 1898 by *The New York Times'* literary and art critic Charles de Kay, the National Arts Club remains an elite, members-only club dedicated to promoting public interest in the fine arts. The club, based in the Tilden Mansion at 15 Gramercy Park, boasts a façade designed by Calvert Vaux. The interior features fireplaces created by skilled Italian wood carvers, as well as stained glass ceilings by John LaFarge. The mansion is designated as both a New York City Landmark and a National Historic Landmark. *Left:* The Hotel Gramercy Park in its earliest incarnation.

Right: The statue of Edwin Booth in Gramercy Park was the first in the city to be dedicated to an actor. Booth was well known for his Shakespearean roles; unfortunately, he is also remembered as the brother of President Abraham Lincoln's assassin, the notorious John Wilkes Booth.

Below: Visitors stroll through Madison Square Park in the late 1800s.

Left: Pete's Tavern has remained open for more than 140 years—even during Prohibition, when it was disguised as a floral shop.

MADISON SQUARE GARDEN

Today's Madison Square Garden, located at 7th Avenue between 31st and 33rd streets, is the fourth incarnation of various arenas with the same name. The first stood on 23rd Street and Madison Avenue in a former passenger depot transformed by circus showman P. T. Barnum into "Barnum's Monster Classical and Geological Hippodrome." The building was later renamed Madison Square Garden after its location.

In 1891, a new Madison Square Garden, designed by architect Stanford White, rose on the same site. Boasting the largest American amphitheater, it held 8,000 seats. The venue's Moorish architecture featured colonnades and a soaring tower resembling a minaret. A naked statue of the goddess Diana topped the Garden, causing quite a stir at the time.

White kept an apartment in the tower. While in his late 40s (and married), he seduced Evelyn Nesbit, a teenage chorus girl and artist's model known as one of the iconic "Gibson Girls." She later married millionaire Harry Kendall Thaw, who learned about her previous affair with White. In 1906, Thaw, mad with jealousy, shot and killed White at a performance at the Garden's roof theater. This original "Trial of the Century" ended with a "not guilty" verdict for Thaw by reason of insanity.

A third Madison Square Garden opened in 1925 on 8th Avenue and 50th Street, and finally, in 1968, the present-day arena was built on the site of Pennsylvania Station's street level. The four-block-long station, built in 1910, was designed by McKim, Mead and White. In 1963, its pink granite columns and 15-story high waiting room, inspired by opulent Roman bathhouses, were torn down amid protests. The current Penn Station was relocated beneath Madison Square Garden.

Currently, the Garden can provide seating for nearly 20,000 spectators. The New York Knicks and the New York Rangers currently call the Garden home. The arena hosts more than 300 events annually, including concerts by popular musicians such as Bon Jovi, Christina Aguilera, and Beyoncé.

Above: The first Madison Square Garden featured a velodrome for bicycle racing. The venue was demolished in 1889 and replaced two years later by a second venue *(shown right),* built by architect Stanford White, on the same site.

The Garden's Many Faces

Left: The third incarnation of Madison Square Garden, shown here in 1943, was a popular destination. The marquee advertises a rodeo championship featuring an appearance by the "King of Cowboys," Roy Rogers.

A large clock (below left) heralded this concourse in the old Pennsylvania Station in 1962. When plans were made to level the old Pennsylvania Station (seen below in 1910) to make way for a new Madison Square Garden in 1963, outcries were heard from many prestigious groups and the public alike, including the American Institute of Architects (AIA), but to no avail.

Present-day Madison Square Garden, as seen from its 8th Avenue entrance. Thanks to its ingenious design by R. E. McKee, the Garden was the first such structure to be built upon an active railroad station and system.

MACY'S HERALD SQUARE

The area where Broadway and 6th Avenue converge at 34th Street and its surrounding vicinity is called Herald Square. It received its name in the mid-1800s, when the *New York Herald* newspaper had its headquarters here. Now, Herald Square's most famous resident is Macy's, which has proclaimed itself the largest department store in the world since 1924.

Founded by Rowland Hussey Macy in 1858, R. H. Macy's was based in several buildings, including one in the former Ladies' Mile section of upscale retail establishments. In 1902, Macy moved his flagship store to its current Herald Square location, starting with one building and then expanding as his sales increased.

Since its inception in 1924, the annual Macy's Thanksgiving Day Parade has become a famous store—and city—tradition. The festivities begin at 77th Street, and the parade wends its way down Manhattan's streets, with marching bands, entertainers, and elaborate floats entertaining thousands of spectators. Gigantic helium balloons soar overhead, featuring characters such as a looming Shrek and a huge Flying Ace Snoopy.

The store also presents its annual Macy's Fourth of July Fireworks Spectacular. Each year, millions watch as four barges on the East River send up fireworks that light up the sky from 23rd Street to 42nd Street. Since 1980, a section of Macy's eighth floor has been home to the De Gustibus cooking school, known for its tagline, "The School of Good Taste."

R. H. Macy opened the first Macy's store on 6th Avenue in the fashionable Ladies' Mile district in 1880. *Inset:* Fashion-conscious woman in the early 1900s had their pick of Macy's hats, including the "Stylish High Crown Sailor" design, a "Mushroom Turban," and other hats that seem heavy and unwieldy by today's standards.

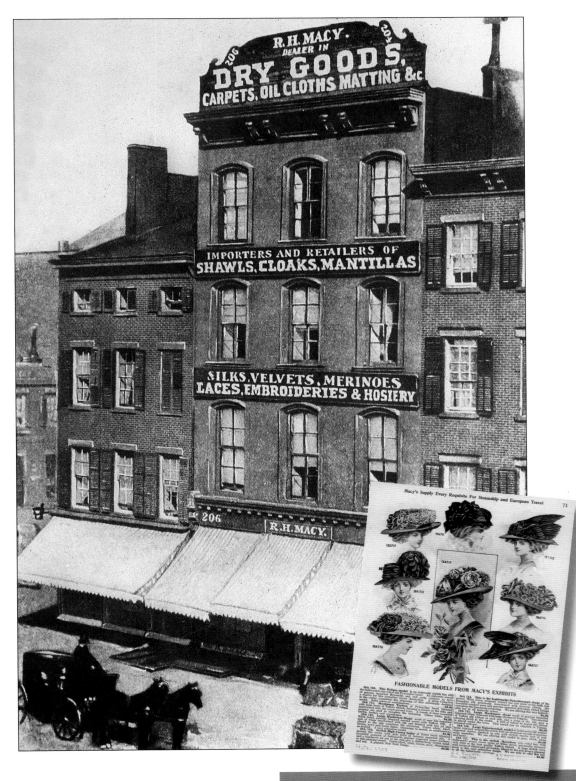

Herald Square

In the late 1800s and early 1900s, Herald Square (left) teemed with trolley cars, horse-drawn carriages, and pedestrians. Above the street, an elevated railroad roared past the area. Today the area remains a busy thoroughfare, as seen below. Although Macy's stores are located as far away as Hawaii and Guam, the flagship store remains the one in Herald Square.

Below: Since 1924, crowds have lined up for the annual Macy's Thanksgiving Day parade. Here, a Captain Nemo balloon makes its way down the street in 1929.

Left: Traditional and contemporary architectural elements blend seamlessly at the present-day Morgan Library & Museum. *Above:* A portrait of John P. Morgan Sr. hangs on a wall above the fireplace in the West Room of the Morgan Library & Museum in 1945.

THE MORGAN LIBRARY & MUSEUM

During his lifetime, financier Pierpont Morgan only invited the elite into his stately home on 36th Street and Madison Avenue, but after his death, his son J. P. opened Morgan's library to the public. Built between 1902 and 1906, just east of the Morgan family's residence, the library housed the financier's extraordinary collection of paintings, drawings, and rare books. Charles F. McKim, of the renowned architectural firm of McKim, Mead and White, designed the library.

In 1924, J. P. transformed the building from a private retreat into a public library to be enjoyed by all. Several additions increased the institution's size throughout the years. The Annex was added in 1928 when the Morgans' brownstone residence was razed to the ground and a new building erected.

In 2000, architect Renzo Piano was hired to enhance the Morgan. The renovated complex features a new concert hall and a glass-enclosed courtyard. As before, the institution exhibits its trove of masterpieces, including an original musical score by Mozart and the only surviving manuscript of John Milton's epic poem "Paradise Lost."

The Morgan Library & Museum boasts three Gutenberg Bibles. There are only 50 surviving copies in the world.

New York is easily identified by its skyline. Even author Kurt Vonnegut Jr. dubbed it "Skyscraper national park." This photo of the iconic New York skyline in 1939 includes the Chrysler building, the Chanin Building, and the Lincoln Building.

SKYSCRAPERS

Since the 20th century, NYC's fame has been linked to its dramatic skyline. What transformed Manhattan from a low-lying island to a vertical city were two 19th-century innovations: steel cage construction and the invention of elevators. When the Fuller Building, best known as the Flatiron Building, rose to 307 feet in 1903, it was considered an engineering marvel. Many consider it NYC's first skyscraper. The northern end features a rounded tip that burgeons into a triangular shape. Looming like a gigantic pressing iron, the building fit perfectly into the plot on which it was built between Broadway, 5th Avenue, and 23rd Street.

Another iconic skyscraper, the Chrysler Building, built in 1930, rises 77 floors, then tapers into a pointed sunburst pattern with massive triangular windows. Eclectic decorations such as hubcaps and stylized eagles adorn the building, while the lobby is lined with marble walls and ornate elevator doors. Artist Edward Trumbull's expansive murals of progress in transportation grace the ceiling.

Perhaps the best-known skyscraper, the Empire State Building, was described by writer F. Scott Fitzgerald as rising "from the ruins" of the original Waldorf=Astoria Hotel, "lonely and inexplicable as the sphinx." Built in 1931, the 102-story structure was the tallest building in the world for over four decades until the World Trade Center's North Tower surpassed it in 1972. After the September 11 attacks destroyed the Twin Towers, the Empire State Building was once again NYC's tallest skyscraper.

In the 1960s, the city saw a renewed interest in building skyscrapers. Today, soaring structures such as the eco-friendly Hearst Magazine Building, the Time Warner Center, and the Trump World Tower enhance the city's skyline.

Legend has it that the term "23 Skidoo," an early 20th-century term meaning "Get lost," started with the Flatiron Building, seen here in 1910. As the story goes, the area is rather windy, and when construction workers on the building ogled women whose skirts flew up, policemen would yell "23 Skidoo!" to get the men to stop looking and leave. *Right:* William Van Alen designed the archetypical Art Deco skyscraper, the Chrysler Building. Born in Brooklyn, Van Alen later studied in Paris at the École des Beaux-Arts. He incorporated what he learned in France into his monumental design for the Chrysler Building.

Color Coded

The Empire State Building (pictured above) soars above the New York City skyline. At night, different colors illuminate the structure, and each color has a special meaning. On Frank Sinatra's birthday, the building is bathed in a blue light for "Old Blue Eyes"; on March 17, the color green celebrates St. Patrick's Day. Unfortunately, during bird migration seasons, the bright lights can attract the birds, sometimes causing them to slam into the building. If they notice flocks of birds approaching, observatory personnel on the 86th floor will turn off the lights on the top floor.

THE NEW YORK PUBLIC LIBRARY AND BRYANT PARK

Library Lions

Designed by American sculptor Edward Clark Potter and carved by the Piccirilli brothers, the two lions in front of the New York Public Library building on 42nd Street have attained iconic status. The marble animals were at first nicknamed "Leo Astor" and "Leo Lenox" in honor of the two public libraries that provided the bulk of the book collection. Later, they were called "Lady Astor" and "Lord Lenox," despite the fact that both lions are males. In the 1930s, Mayor Fiorello La Guardia dubbed them "Patience" (seen here) and "Fortitude," their names to this day.

Two well-known stone lions, Patience and Fortitude, stand guard over the New York Public Library, the opulent building on 42nd Street and 5th Avenue. With a collection of almost 50 million items, including books, rare manuscripts, and maps, the NYPL is one of the world's foremost research libraries. It boasts a number of rare treasures, including Washington Irving's handwritten notebooks and the first Gutenberg Bible to arrive in the United States. The library includes over 80 branches, all of which are open to the public.

Originally established from the private libraries of James Lenox and John Jacob Astor, with additional funding by Samuel J. Tilden, the building opened in 1911 on the site of the former Croton Distributing Reservoir. At the time, it was the largest marble building in the United States; its Main Reading Room alone stretches nearly 300 feet, with ornate chandeliers and high windows shedding light over the vast space.

Just behind the library, present-day Bryant Park provides a quiet respite from the surrounding taller buildings. A potter's field until 1840, the park was initially dubbed Reservoir Square after the former reservoir to the east.

In 1853, the Crystal Palace opened in the park, built to house New York's first world's fair. A spectacular glass-and-cast-iron building, the design was inspired by London's original Crystal Palace. Despite attendance by over one million visitors, the fair closed the following year. The palace was then leased out for gala events. Although promoted as fireproof, the building burned to the ground in 1858. In 1884, the park was renamed in honor of poet, editor, and reformer William Cullen Bryant.

By the 1970s, the area grew seedy as drug dealers and the homeless frequented the park. In 1992, the park underwent renovation. Now with verdant trees, promenades, and a carousel, Bryant Park hosts concerts in the summer and a skating rink in the winter.

Left: When the New York Crystal Palace opened in 1853, a *New York Times* article remarked, "The nations meet, not in war, but in peace, beneath this dome."

Left: The library's Main Reading Room. *Right:* Two men play chess in Bryant Park, with a statue of industrialist, congressman, and YMCA member William Earle Dodge in the background.

Rays of sunlight stream from lofty windows into Grand Central's main concourse in this photo from the 1930s.

GRAND CENTRAL TERMINAL

Although New Yorkers usually call the cavernous space "Grand Central Station," this NYC landmark is technically a terminal. The magnificent Beaux Arts–style building is not the first to bear the Grand Central name and occupy this site, however. Cornelius Vanderbilt opened his Grand Central Depot in 1871; after it was enlarged in 1898, it was called Grand Central Station.

Public outcry over a disastrous train collision in 1902 led to the demolition of that station, and plans were made for a new terminal for trains powered by electricity. On February 2, 1913, a jubilant crowd of 150,000 visitors came to the newly opened (and renamed) Grand Central Terminal. Soon after, hotels and skyscrapers rose around the bustling station.

Grand Central boasts a Grand Staircase modeled after one in the former Paris Opera House. Crystal chandeliers, marble floors, and a lofty ceiling painted to resemble celestial constellations create an air of elegance throughout.

The most recognizable element here is the large clock sitting atop the information booth. Each of the clock's four faces is crafted of opal; the timepiece has an estimated worth of $10 to $20 million.

Secrets abound at Grand Central, including the mysterious (and now abandoned) Track 61. The line was used to transport President Franklin Roosevelt to and from his Hyde Park home, so as to hide his disabilities from the public. Meanwhile, near the Oyster Bar, curved arches create what is called the Whispering Wall, known for its trick acoustics. There, if someone whispers into a corner, the sound is heard in the opposite corner.

Above: In 1914, French sculptor Jules Coutan created this massive limestone sculptural grouping of Roman deities centered around a clock. Mercury represents commerce, and the surrounding figures of Minerva and Hercules denote mental and moral strength. A *New York Times* article from that era described the sculptor as holding a "poor opinion of American art."

Above: Grand Central Terminal, as seen from the corner of East 42nd Street and Vanderbilt Avenue in 1937. At right is the Commodore Hotel, named for "Commodore" Cornelius Vanderbilt. That building is now the Grand Hyatt Hotel. *Right:* The Grand Central Oyster Bar & Restaurant opened in 1913 on the lower level of the station. Its elegant décor with curved archways and ceiling tiles has hosted commuters and celebrities alike. Known for its seafood and famous raw bar, the restaurant has endured through the years. After a fire destroyed a great deal of the restaurant in 1997, the venue was restored to its former grandeur.

THE UNITED NATIONS

In 1944, representatives of four countries, including the United States, met at the Dumbarton Oaks conference in Washington, D.C.; there they agreed to found an organization called the United Nations, a successor to the League of Nations.

On October 24, 1945, the new organization was officially established. The General Assembly was first housed in the New York City Building—a remnant of the 1939 World's Fair in Queens—from 1946 until moving to its present headquarters along the East River in 1950. Between 1947 and 1953, an international team of architects including Le Corbusier, Oscar Niemeyer, and Sven Markelius created the concept for the permanent headquarters. American architect Wallace K. Harrison's firm worked with the team to execute the plan.

The dominating structure in the complex, the 39-story Secretariat Building looms over the East River. Although the complex is located on an 18-acre site in NYC, it is considered an international territory. The United Nations also boasts an extensive international art collection. Two large-scale Fernand Léger murals grace the General Assembly Hall, while Barbara Hepworth's sculpture *Single Form* stands by an ornamental pool.

In 2006, the U.N. General Assembly approved allocating funds for a comprehensive renovation to continue from 2007 through 2013 to repair and update the buildings and to meet modern fire and security standards.

Above: A meeting of the General Assembly in 2002 brought together (from back left) former U.N. Secretary-General Kofi Annan, Jan Kavan of the Czech Republic, and Han Seung-soo of Korea. In the center is Kaspar Villiger of Switzerland. *Left:* The United Nations building faces the East River, adding to Manhattan's many towering structures.

THE *INTREPID* SEA, AIR & SPACE MUSEUM

A true survivor, the U.S.S. *Intrepid* aircraft carrier lived through five kamikaze attacks during World War II and went on to hold its own during the Korean and Vietnam wars. Even so, the 36,000-ton vessel, which spans the length of three football fields, was narrowly saved from the scrap yard.

But in 1978, philanthropist Zachary Fisher and his wife, Elizabeth, worked hard to save the vessel. In 1982, docked in the Hudson River at Pier 86 on 46th Street, the *Intrepid* opened once again, this time as a floating museum. Millions have since come aboard the historic ship, making it one of the top five tourist attractions in New York City.

In 2006, the *Intrepid* left its Manhattan home for nearly two years of restoration, and on November 8, 2008, it reopened to the public. The national icon now boasts a collection of 30 refurbished historic aircraft. There is also a new 13,000-square-foot Explorium hands-on learning center for children. Here, young visitors can climb inside a re-creation of the original *Gemini III* space capsule, which was recovered by the *Intrepid* in 1965.

Above: Among the *Intrepid*'s aircraft collection is a Grumman F-11 Tiger. The U.S. Navy's flight demonstration team, the Blue Angels, flew Tigers from 1957 until 1968. *Left:* The U.S.S. *Intrepid* makes its way through the waters off Guantanamo Bay, Cuba, in 1955.

TIMES SQUARE

Originally known as Longacre Square, the area centering on the junction of Broadway, 7th Avenue, and 42nd Street was a respectable, affluent neighborhood in the early 19th century. The rich and powerful, including the Astors and the Vanderbilts, either lived or did business there. By the late 1800s, however, exclusive brothels also shared the neighborhood.

Soon, the square became known for its various forms of entertainment: Theaters started moving here from their former downtown hub, and in 1904, *The New York Times* moved to a new building in the square. From then on, the district was known as Times Square. The newspaper has moved twice since then, but it has always stayed in the general area.

By the late '20s, more than 70 theaters were producing hundreds of shows on Broadway near Times Square. But the Great Depression hit hard, and the district devolved into rows of theaters screening pornographic movies. No longer an up-and-coming place, now peep shows, drug dealing, and prostitution reigned. In the 1960s and '70s, Times Square was infamous for its high crime rate. By the 1980s, however, a group now known as the Times Square Alliance spearheaded a redevelopment movement, which included the renovation of former theaters.

The New Year's Eve dropping of a lighted ball from the original *New York Times* building remains a Times Square tradition. Since the first time the ball was lit atop a flagpole on One Times Square in 1907, millions of onlookers have braved the freezing weather to glimpse the symbol of the arrival of the New Year. On New Year's Eve 2008, the event's organizers unveiled a new, sparkling 12-foot geodesic sphere that weighs more than 11,000 pounds.

In 1900, Broadway and 42nd Street was a busy intersection. Every available space was filled with advertisements for upcoming shows and goods for sale. While it was still called Longacre Square, the area was known for being the center of the carriage industry. Years later, the New York-to-Paris "Greatest Auto Race" of 1908 began here.

Above: The 1930s were rough for everyone because of the Great Depression. Despite the slump, Times Square blossomed with the availability of neon lighting. Advertising aces such as Douglas Leigh produced some of their best work during this era. *Left:* In 1908, the former Times Building in Times Square towered over the neighborhood.

Over the years, Times Square has been known for its grime as well as its glitz. After former Mayor Rudy Giuliani instituted a cleanup of Times Square in the 1990s, the area is milder, though no less dazzling.

A New Home

In 2007, *The New York Times* moved into its new building at 620 8th Avenue, a 52-story tower designed by award-winning architect Renzo Piano in association with FXFOWLE Architects. Piano said he wanted a "transparent relationship between the street and the building"; he achieved that end with ample glass walls in his design. The building also features a number of sustainable design elements including a shading system that saves 30 percent in energy costs. The *Times* offices occupy the first 27 floors. The building also houses TheTimesCenter, a cultural center and performance space.

BROADWAY

Twentieth-century Irish dramatist Sean O'Casey called Broadway a "wide wonder" that becomes "gaudily glorious at night." But the original inhabitants of Manhattan, the Lenape, called the long trail they had built the Wickquasgeck Trail. It wended its way on top of a natural ridge running north and south along the length of Manhattan Island. When the Dutch arrived, they made the street wider and called it Gentlemen's Street. The British later dubbed it Broadway because of its ample width.

Today, the very name conjures up visions of entertaining shows—with raucous choruses and vivacious dancers—that attract mostly tourists to the Theater District's many long-running musicals. Although most of the modern theaters were built on side streets near (not on) the famed avenue, people still refer to productions there as "Broadway shows."

In 1866, a French ballet company was brought to New York but found themselves without a venue. The troupe approached William Wheatley, manager of the 3,000-seat Niblo's Garden, then located on Broadway and Prince Street. Wheatley's upcoming show, a melodrama called *The Black Crook*, featured a plot similar to Goethe's *Faust*. The troupe pitched the idea of combining their dancing with Wheatley's show—the birth of the Broadway musical. Although the show lasted a mind-numbing 5½ hours, it still ran for a record-breaking 474 performances.

Today's Theater District features Broadway shows in approximately 40 theaters. Off-Broadway shows are performed in venues with less than 500 seats, and off-off-Broadway theaters are smaller still, with accommodations for less than 99 ticket holders.

Top: The Orpheum Dance Palace was a fixture at Broadway and 48th Street, as seen here in 1937. *Middle:* A 1927 poster advertises the original production of Jerome Kern and Oscar Hammerstein's Broadway musical *Show Boat. Bottom:* Theater fans can find something for every palate, from classic musicals to new undertakings. Wild 1980s London is brought back in the musical *Taboo,* which played at the Plymouth Theatre, as seen here in 2003. Pop icon Boy George performed in the show.

ROCKEFELLER CENTER

The stock market crash of 1929 destroyed many dreams, but John D. Rockefeller Jr. pursued his vision for the area from 49th Street to 52nd Street, bounded by 5th and 6th avenues. Holding a 24-year lease on the $91 million property, he had originally planned to build, among other things, a new Metropolitan Opera House on the site. But after Black Tuesday, the Met couldn't afford the move. Instead, he decided to construct a grand plaza with an office-building complex. Opened in 1933, Rockefeller Center was considered the largest private building project in modern times.

The grandeur and elegance that Rockefeller envisioned for his Art Deco project remains to this day in its 19 buildings and plaza. At the heart of the complex lies 30 Rockefeller Center, with its Top of the Rock three-level observation deck. Now renovated and offering spectacular 360-degree panoramas behind transparent safety glass, Top of the Rock's outdoor space is open 365 days a year.

Millions of visitors have admired the golden statue of Prometheus overlooking the ice skating rink in winter, which is converted into an outdoor eating area in the summer. A towering tree is the centerpiece of the center's annual Christmas celebration.

Located within Rockefeller Center, Radio City Music Hall is the world's largest indoor theater, and its stage boasts the world's largest curtain, which shimmers in a glistening gold color. The annual *Radio City Christmas Spectacular* entertains with music and dancing by the world-famous, high-kicking Rockettes. Modern and classic movies have opened at Radio City, from the original *King Kong* to *The Lion King*.

Skaters whirl around the ice skating rink in Rockefeller Center. The famous statue of Prometheus and a lighted Christmas tree glow in the background.

Above: The Top of the Rock Observation Deck allows visitors jaw-dropping views of Manhattan 365 days a year. The original observatory opened in 1933, but remained closed for decades until the restored, redesigned deck opened in 2005. *Right:* In 1982, the Radio City Music Hall Rockettes danced on 6th Avenue to celebrate the hall's 50th anniversary. The Rockettes were formed in 1925 by Russell Markert, who wanted dancers who could kick their legs at least six inches over their heads.

SAINT PATRICK'S CATHEDRAL

The idea of a magnificent Gothic-style cathedral was at first ridiculed when Archbishop John Hughes (a.k.a. "Dagger John" because of his reputation as a man not to double cross) first proposed his vision in 1853 for a huge Catholic house of worship. Hughes, the first archbishop of New York, hoped to build a cathedral in the city, "worthy of our increasing numbers, intelligence and wealth as a religious community…and worthy as a public architectural monument."

At the time, the area he spoke of (between present-day 50th and 51st streets and 5th Avenue) was considered far from the existing city and was largely undeveloped. Detractors referred to the idea of a grand cathedral in such an unworthy area as "Hughes' Folly." But the Irish-born archbishop persisted, and thanks to 103 donors who gave $1,000 each—and the smaller donations from thousands of poor Irish immigrants—Dagger John's dream finally became a reality when the doors of Saint Patrick's Cathedral opened in 1879.

Saint Patrick's predecessor, now known as Old Saint Patrick's, was dedicated in 1815 on Mulberry Street, where it stands to this day. The former seat of the Roman Catholic Archdiocese of New York, the building ceded that title with the opening of the current Saint Patrick's in 1879; today Old Saint Patrick's functions as a parish church.

A National Historic Landmark, Saint Patrick's gleaming white marble walls support two soaring, 330-foot spires, punctuated with stained-glass creations such as the awe-inspiring Rose Window. Visitors are greeted by massive 20,000-pound bronze doors that feature American saints. Funeral masses have been held in the cathedral for various celebrities including politician Robert F. Kennedy, baseball legend Babe Ruth, and Cuban singer Celia Cruz.

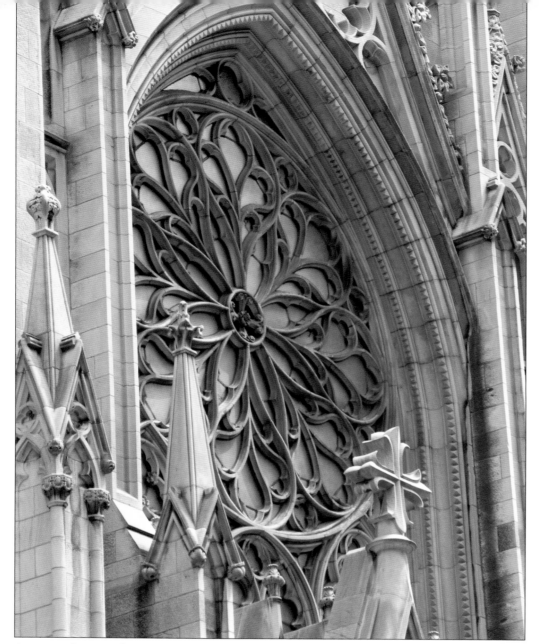

Saint Patrick's magnificent Rose Window was crafted by American painter and stained-glass artist Charles Connick. It is considered one of his masterpieces.

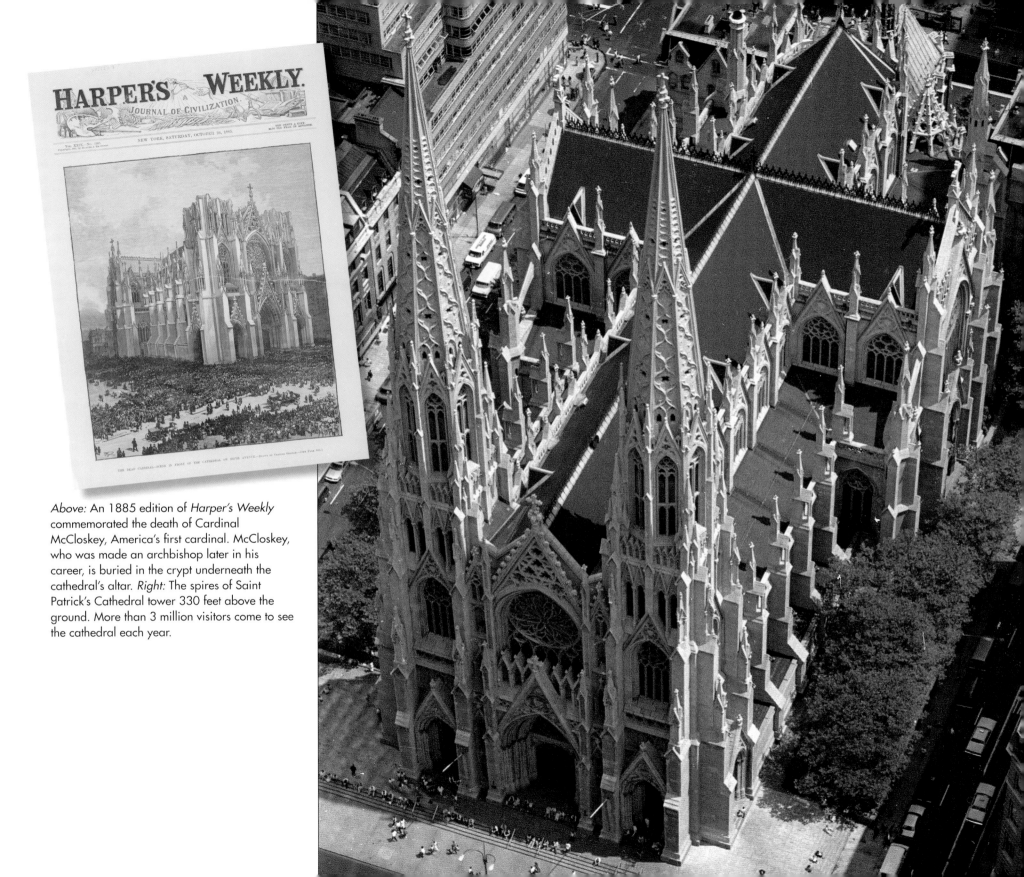

Above: An 1885 edition of *Harper's Weekly* commemorated the death of Cardinal McCloskey, America's first cardinal. McCloskey, who was made an archbishop later in his career, is buried in the crypt underneath the cathedral's altar. *Right:* The spires of Saint Patrick's Cathedral tower 330 feet above the ground. More than 3 million visitors come to see the cathedral each year.

Above: In this humorous photo, circa 1930, construction workers on the Waldorf=Astoria Hotel enjoy lunch served on platters as they sit precariously high above the city streets. *Right:* The Waldorf=Astoria at its old location (now the site of the Empire State Building), circa 1901.

THE WALDORF=ASTORIA HOTEL

The legendary Waldorf=Astoria Hotel on Park Avenue, between 49th and 50th streets, remains one of the most significant Art Deco buildings in the world. The famed venue initially was two separate hotels founded by different members of the prestigious Astor family. In 1893, William Waldorf Astor opened his 13-story Waldorf Hotel on 5th Avenue and 33rd Street. John Jacob Astor IV outdid his cousin by building his adjacent Astoria Hotel four stories higher.

Finally, in 1897 the two hotels became one, joined by a corridor dubbed "Peacock Alley."

The double hyphen in the new hotel's name, the Waldorf=Astoria, came to represent the connection between the buildings. In 1929, the two buildings were razed, and the site became the home of the Empire State Building.

In 1931, the current Waldorf=Astoria opened as the largest and tallest hotel in the world at the time. It boasted electricity and private bathrooms in many rooms, which at the time were two very special amenities. Also, single women did not have to use a private entrance, as was the custom at most hotels. The Waldorf was also the first to

institute room service. The Waldorf's presidential suite has hosted every U.S. president since 1931. Other famous guests include inventor Nikola Tesla, actress Marilyn Monroe, and the infamous mobster "Lucky" Luciano.

Arguably the most famous employee of the hotel was the maître d'hôtel, Oscar Tschirky, known as "Oscar of the Waldorf." In 1896, he created the Waldorf salad, combining diced red-skinned apples, celery, and mayonnaise (and later, chopped walnuts), which continues to delight generations of food aficionados.

Above: Famous guests who walked through the doors of the Waldorf=Astoria have included Cole Porter, Douglas MacArthur, and Prince Rainier and Princess Grace of Monaco.

Left: The Waldorf=Astoria's lobby features a large clock created by Goldsmith's Company, London, for the 1893 Chicago World's Fair. The timepiece was later bought by the Astor family. The clock's base features portraits of Queen Victoria and several American presidents. Its chimes replicate the sound of Westminster Cathedral's clock tower in London.

THE MUSEUM OF MODERN ART

Within these walls, Van Gogh's *Starry Night* glitters, and graceful women frolic in Matisse's *Dance*. From Pablo Picasso to Georges Braque and Amedeo Modigliani, the Museum of Modern Art comprises one of the most widely ranging collections of contemporary creations, including painting, sculpture, photography, video, film, and furniture.

Conceived by Miss Lillie P. Bliss, Mrs. Cornelius J. Sullivan, and Mrs. John D. Rockefeller Jr., three patrons of the arts, the museum held exhibits in various venues from 1929 until it moved to its current home in 1939. MoMA started out with a modest gift of eight prints and one drawing, but since then, its collection has grown to a vast holding of more than 150,000 works of art, as well as four mil-lion film stills and 22,000 films. The museum's research library boasts more than 300,000 books and periodicals.

Through the years, millions of visitors have enjoyed masterpieces from the permanent collection. Changing exhibits have brought to the viewing public artworks by artists including Joan Miró, Edouard Manet, Paul Klee, and others.

In 2002, the museum closed for renovations. It reopened in 2004 with nearly double the size of the original building and the extended Abby Aldrich Rockefeller Sculpture Garden, now home to Richard Serra creations. The museum also houses a gourmet restaurant, where sophisticated fare awaits visitors after their tour of modern masterpieces.

MoMA's outdoor sculpture garden hosts live concerts as well as artwork. Above, *Moonbird*, a bronze sculpture by Joan Miró, represents the meshing of male and female, as well as the sun and moon.

Right: The museum's galleries are home to paintings, sculpture, photography, and more, including work by Jackson Pollock (pictured). *Opposite:* The Museum of Modern Art has captivated visitors with its soaring architecture and vast collections.

FIFTH AVENUE

The very mention of the name "Fifth Avenue" conjures up images of millionaires' apartments and upscale boutiques. With prestigious addresses come pricey rents and wares: In 2008, *Forbes* magazine pronounced this the world's most expensive street.

The avenue that begins at Washington Square Park in the West Village runs northward all the way up to the Harlem River at 142nd Street. It divides Manhattan's addresses into east and west, as the numbers adjacent to either side of the avenue start low, but increase as streets lie farther and farther away.

In the 1800s, millionaire families such as the Astors and the Vanderbilts built their mansions along the avenue, giving it a cachet that has lasted until the present. In the 1920s and '30s, upscale department stores such as Saks Fifth Avenue transformed a residential area into an opulent shopping district as well.

Fifth Avenue is home to noted structures such as the Empire State Building, Saint Patrick's Cathedral, the New York Public Library, and Rockefeller Center. Among the stores lining the avenue are legendary jewelers Tiffany & Co., as well as high-fashion venues such as Gucci and Prada.

The avenue also provides a route for many parades, including the Puerto Rican Parade and the Italian-themed Columbus Day Parade.

ROOSEVELT ISLAND

As the tram ascends from 59th Street and 2nd Avenue to a height of 250 feet, passengers glimpse a vast panorama of the East River below. Within four minutes, they are transported from Manhattan's traffic to the quieter streets of Roosevelt Island. Before a bridge from Queens opened in 1955, and the 1976 opening of the only aerial commuter tram in the United States, visitors reached the island via rowboats, ferries, or trolleys running across the Queensboro Bridge. Since 1989, the F train tunnels under the river to connect the boroughs.

Roosevelt Island evolved into a residential community in the 1970s, and it now features apartment buildings, landscaped parks, and minimal amounts of traffic. In its storied past, the two-mile-long island was called Minnahannock by the Native Americans, then Hog's Island by the Dutch, who raised pigs on the farmland. The island was also known as Blackwell's Island, Welfare Island, and finally, Roosevelt Island.

In the past, farms, an almshouse, and an orphanage have all had residence on the island. The Blackwell Island Penitentiary opened in 1832; among the inmates passing through its locked doors were the infamous New York gangster Dutch Schultz and sultry actress Mae West, who spent ten days in jail there after appearing in her scandalous play, *Sex*.

The New York Lunatic Asylum opened in 1839. Pioneer investigative journalist Nellie Bly faked insanity and was committed there for a horrific ten days. Her scathing articles about the asylum's unsanitary and abusive conditions led to social reform.

Top: When Charles Dickens took a tour of the infamous mental hospital on Blackwell's Island in 1842 (later called Roosevelt Island, seen here in 1970), he noted that "everything [at the asylum] had a lounging, listless, madhouse air which was very painful." *Bottom:* High above the East River, the Roosevelt Island Tramway brings visitors to and from the island.

MOVING ON UP

Until the mid-1800s, most of Manhattan above 59th Street—now generally referred to as Uptown Manhattan—was undeveloped, with farms here and there, empty lots, and an occasional town such as Harlem in the north. Originally settled by the Dutch in the 1600s, and named New Haarlem after their native city, the town's name was changed to Harlem by the British when they seized the land. The Dyckman Farmhouse Museum is an example of an original Dutch farmhouse built in the late 1700s. Standing on present-day Broadway and 204th Street, it remains one of the oldest structures from the time of New Amsterdam.

In 1802, Alexander Hamilton—advisor to George Washington during the American Revolution and the first Secretary of the United States Treasury—settled in his home, Hamilton Grange in West Harlem, where he lived until his death. It's now known as the Hamilton Grange National Memorial. As part of the National Park system, the house has been moved twice; it reopened not far from its original location in 2009.

But Harlem wasn't all manors and sprawling estates. There were also shantytowns, populated by indigent German and Irish immigrants, as well as a squatters' camp near present-day West 82nd Street. This area was called Seneca Village, where poor blacks, Native Americans, and impoverished immigrants made their homes in ramshackle huts; some even took shelter in natural caves.

These areas were eventually torn down. In fact, more than 1,000 residents lost their homes when the city decided to build the nation's first public park, Central Park, which opened in the winter of 1859.

CLASS DIVISION

As Central Park's 843 acres became a quiet urban oasis for both upper- and lower-class New Yorkers, new neighborhoods sprang up near the park in the late 19th century. Along the eastern and western

Opposite: Boaters in 1894 enjoy a view of the Bethesda Fountain, with its famous statue of the *Angel of the Waters.*

The Russian Ballet (seen here in 1942) performed in the first Metropolitan Opera House on Broadway and 39th Street. The Met was founded by a group of businessmen who wanted their own opera house. Today's Met, however, is far more inclusive.

borders of Central Park, the Upper East and the Upper West Sides developed.

By the turn of the century, an enormous class division developed between the poor, who lived in crowded housing in places such as the Lower East Side, and the very wealthy, many of whom built palatial residences on 5th Avenue alongside the rolling green expanses of Central Park. Known as Millionaire's Row, this extravagant stretch of New York City included the four-story, 64-room mansion built in 1901 for Scottish-born industrialist Andrew Carnegie. Equipped with the latest in then-modern technology, the mansion boasted central heating and an elevator. Today the imposing structure is home to the Cooper-Hewitt National Design Museum.

Not to be outdone, in 1914, steel industrialist Henry Clay Frick moved into an even more grandiose mansion on 5th Avenue and 70th Street. The Frick home was designed to serve as a magnificent residence as well as a repository for the millionaire's impressive art collection. After the deaths of Frick and his wife, the mansion was eventually transformed into The Frick Collection, a museum that continues to exist for the enjoyment of art lovers.

By the 1870s, the elevated trains that connected many parts of the city were expanded farther to the north, including the 9th Avenue el on the Upper West Side. The addition allowed people to live in Uptown Manhattan and still commute to Midtown and Downtown areas.

Facing Central Park's western flank, The Dakota opened on 72nd Street in 1884 as New York City's first luxury apartment house. The building became famous in its own right: In the 1968 horror film *Rosemary's Baby*, actress Mia Farrow enters The Dakota during one of the movie's opening scenes. The street in front of the building was also the site of John Lennon's murder on the evening of December 8, 1980, as he came home to his apartment. Other famous residents of The Dakota include actor Boris Karloff, actress Lauren Bacall, and composer Leonard Bernstein.

UPTOWN EXPANDS

Areas such as Morningside Heights, Washington Heights, Inwood, and Harlem also developed as increased train coverage made these northern Manhattan areas more accessible. At the turn of the century, Harlem was considered a middle-class neighborhood; it underwent many transformations until it became the center of African American culture in New York City.

Morningside Heights (from West 110th Street to West 125th Street) abuts

An arched bridge sets an idyllic scene in Central Park. The green space harbors 36 bridges and arches, seven ornamental fountains, and more than 26,000 trees.

Harlem, and it is home to Columbia University's campus, as well as the still-unfinished Cathedral of St. John the Divine. Grant's Tomb, the resting place of the former president and his wife, is another of the area's highlights.

MODERN UPTOWN
In the 1960s, the Lincoln Center for the Performing Arts opened its complex of theaters and concert halls. These include the Avery Fisher Hall, La Guardia Concert Hall, Alice Tully Hall,

the Metropolitan Opera House, and more. One of the foremost performing arts centers in the country, the complex is located on Manhattan's Upper West Side, between West 62nd and West 65th streets, and Columbus and Amsterdam avenues. The open-air venue, Damrosch Park, also hosts the Lincoln Center Out of Doors series every summer, when visitors can enjoy performances of a wide variety of musical styles, puppet shows, and dance performances, all free and open to the public.

In the late 1990s, the Harlem neighborhood underwent a gentrification phase, and many former brownstones were renovated and sold at high prices. When former president Bill Clinton left the White House, he set up his office on 125th Street in Harlem. In 2006, construction began on West Harlem Piers Park, built on the site of former piers that were demolished in the 1950s. In 2008, it opened to the public, helping to return the area to the thriving waterfront of its past.

In the evening, the lights of the Guggenheim Museum illuminate its unique shape, as seen in this photo from 1960.

CARNEGIE HALL

When the cornerstone of Carnegie Hall was laid in place in 1890, steel magnate and philanthropist Andrew Carnegie said, "It is built to stand for the ages, and it is probable that this hall will intertwine itself with the history of our country." His words proved true; the musical venue that bears his name continues to enthrall audiences.

On opening night, May 5, 1891, the concert hall was packed to capacity. The evening's highlight came as Russian composer Peter Tchaikovsky strode to the podium and conducted his *Marche Solennelle*. Through the years, numerous renowned performers have entertained at Carnegie Hall. Composer and pianist Sergei Rachmaninoff played his Second Piano Concerto there, and opera stars such as Enrico Caruso and Beverly Sills have delighted the hall's audiences. Although racial bias barred African American opera great Marian Anderson from a 1939 performance at the DAR Constitution Hall in Washington, D.C., she was always warmly welcomed to perform at Carnegie Hall.

Originally built to include three auditoriums—the Main Hall, the Chamber Music Hall, and the Recital Hall directly beneath the Main Hall—Carnegie's divisions have changed through the years, but the main venue remains intact. In 2003, Carnegie Hall's Judy and Arthur Zankel Hall opened with room for an audience of nearly 600, and on the third floor, the Joan and Sanford I. Weill Recital Hall, with its 268 seats, is used for more intimate recitals, chamber music performances, and more.

Over a hundred years' worth of famous performers have graced the stages at Carnegie Hall. An old joke tells the story of a tourist who asked, "How do I get to Carnegie Hall?" A New Yorker drolly answered, "Practice, practice, practice."

Left: Educator, author, and African American civil rights advocate Booker T. Washington speaks to a rapt audience during his Tuskegee Institute Silver Anniversary Lecture in 1906. Mark Twain can be seen listening to Washington's speech, seated directly behind him. *Right:* This Carnegie Hall program highlights the 1959-60 season.

The Isaac Stern Auditorium is currently the largest performing space at Carnegie Hall, seating more than 2,800 people. As the late Stern once remarked, "It has been said that the hall itself is an instrument."

COLUMBUS CIRCLE

Today's Columbus Circle is a busy thoroughfare, encircling the point where Broadway, Central Park West, 8th Avenue, and 59th Street converge. In 1892, the circle was named for Christopher Columbus, when Gaetano Russo's statue of the Italian explorer was placed on a tall column of Carrara marble at the intersection's center.

In the past, the area around the present-day circle included San Juan Hill, a tenement-lined neighborhood that at times was host to teeming racial tension. In 1956, Columbus Circle became home to the New York Coliseum, with four floors large enough to host auto and boat

shows and conventions. The Coliseum stood on the site until 2000, when it was demolished to make way for the Time Warner Center, which opened in 2003.

The 55-story, twin-tower Time Warner Center currently dominates the circle; the area surrounding it has gradually turned into an upscale neighborhood. Inside the center are the world headquarters of the Time Warner Corporation, as well as a popular shopping mall with the latest brand-name boutiques.

Restaurants headed by noted chefs, such as Thomas Keller's Per Se and Masa

Takayama's Masa, provide upscale dining that attracts many visitors to the Time Warner Center. The Mandarin Oriental New York, a five-star luxury hotel, occupies the 35th to the 54th floors of the Time Warner Center, built so that all of its rooms offer spectacular views of Manhattan.

In 2008, the Museum of Arts and Design moved into its new, multistoried building at 2 Columbus Circle, more than tripling its original space on 53rd Street. The 12-story building houses over 2,000 objects created from glass, fiber, clay, metal, and wood.

Above: Southwest of Central Park, Columbus Circle was a quieter place in 1907 than it is today. *Right:* With an expansive Whole Foods Market in its basement, multiple upscale restaurants, and designer shops, the Time Warner Center in Columbus Circle also houses a 1,200-seat theater, a hotel, and CNN Studios.

The spectacular new building for the Museum of Arts and Design opened in 2008 in the southwest corner of Columbus Circle. The 54,000-square-foot redesign of an older building features a new textured façade of glazed terra-cotta tile and a contemporary look.

THE METROPOLITAN OPERA

The crowning jewel of the Lincoln Center, the Metropolitan Opera House is renowned as one of the world's finest opera venues. Originally housed on Broadway and 39th Street, that first venue opened in 1883, moving to its current location in 1966.

Offering classic operas of Verdi and Puccini, as well as works by contemporary composers such as Philip Glass, the Met draws 800,000 visitors annually with over 200 performances each season. Chagall murals adorn the opulent front lobby, while Aristide Maillol's bronze statues add to the elegance of the red-carpeted grand staircase. Shimmering Viennese crystal chandeliers gently rise to the glittering golden ceiling before performances begin.

As general manager from 1950 to 1972, Rudolf Bing introduced some of the finest artists of the era, including Maria Callas, Franco Corelli, and Nicolai Gedda. Bing also arranged for the 1955 debut of African American contralto Marian Anderson at a time when racial bias held back many talented individuals. Opera's luminary stars continue to appear at the Met, including Placido Domingo, Luciano Pavarotti, Dmitri Hvorostovsky, Renee Fleming, and Anna Netrebko.

After becoming general manager in 2006, Peter Gelb faced the challenge of adding to the Met's mostly aging audience. To make opera more accessible, his innovative ideas have included hiring Anthony Minghella, director of the film *The English Patient*, to direct Puccini's *Madama Butterfly*. Film director, designer, and producer Franco Zeffirelli worked on the lavish production of Verdi's *La Traviata*. Meanwhile, *The Met: Live in HD* series reaches over 900,000 viewers each season, airing productions in movie theaters around the world and helping to ensure faithful opera fans for decades to come.

Above: A poster announces the Met's Grand Opera 1909–1910 season. *Right:* In 1902, the first Metropolitan Opera House stood at a busy intersection at Broadway and 39th Street.

LINCOLN CENTER FOR THE PERFORMING ARTS

The world's leading performing arts center, Lincoln Center for the Performing Arts graces Manhattan's Upper West Side. It comprises many separate buildings owned by 12 organizations, as well as a library, outdoor venue Damrosch Park, the Juilliard School of dance, drama, and music, and the School of American Ballet. Each year, five million visitors come to Lincoln Center to enjoy symphonies and other performances at the Avery Fisher and Alice Tully halls, opera at the Metropolitan Opera House, and modern riffs at Jazz at Lincoln Center, a member of the complex housed at the nearby Time Warner Center.

But the site wasn't always the center of arts and entertainment. In the late 1950s and early '60s, New York Parks Commissioner Robert Moses chose the center's site in a then run-down section of the city in the hopes of revitalizing the area. (You can see some of the original downtrodden streets in the 1961 film *West Side Story*.) Construction on the 16-acre complex began in 1959, and it opened in 1969.

Among the center's famed venues, the David H. Koch Theater (formerly the New York State Theater) launched the careers of opera luminaries Beverly Sills and Sherrill Milnes, among others. The theater presents the New York City Opera from March through November, when it cedes the space to the New York City Ballet's graceful performances, including the much-loved *Nutcracker Suite*.

In 2006, construction began on the first major revitalization of Lincoln Center, including a new central fountain and an urban grove at 62nd Street. Alice Tully Hall gained an all-glass lobby and an open public space under the Juilliard School's reconstructed exterior and canopy. The transformation was completed to coincide with present-day Lincoln Center's 50th anniversary in 2009–2010.

Lincoln Center's warm glow lights up the night. The Metropolitan Opera House (center) is flanked by the Avery Fisher Hall (right) and the David H. Koch Theater (left).

Ballet Beauty

The New York City Ballet performs one of its best-loved pieces, Tchaikovsky's *Nutcracker Suite,* in 1981. The *Nutcracker* is a holiday tradition for many, including the dancers. One would have to squint to notice, but the bodices of the women's dresses in the "Hot Chocolate" dance sequence are decorated with small cameo pictures of New York City Ballet founders Lincoln Kirstein and George Balanchine.

The Nesuhi Ertegun Jazz Hall of Fame, located inside Jazz at Lincoln Center, honors the iconic musicians who contributed to this genre. Ertegun was a Turkish American record producer and executive at Atlantic Records, known for its jazz recordings of such greats as Charles Mingus and John Coltrane.

THE AMERICAN MUSEUM OF NATURAL HISTORY

In 1869, naturalist Albert Smith Bickmore proposed the creation of a natural history museum. Two years later, exhibits went on view at the museum's first home, the Central Park Arsenal. As more space was needed, the museum moved into a new, permanent home, which opened in 1877 across from Central Park, between West 77th and 81st streets.

Today's American Museum of Natural History continues to educate and entertain visitors of all ages, particularly with its famed Hall of Dinosaurs, where huge skeletons dominate the space. Soaring to a height of five stories, the Barosaurus cast is the world's tallest freestanding dinosaur display.

The Hall of Northwest Coast Indians features massive totem poles depicting hand-carved animals. Four exhibition floors include animal habitat dioramas, many with original background murals by American artist Charles R. Knight. At the age of six, an accident left Knight legally blind, but nevertheless he studied art and went on to become one of the most famous painters of prehistoric animals, particularly dinosaurs.

In 2003, the Milstein Hall of Ocean Life opened after a large renovation. Suspended from the high ceiling, the hall's centerpiece remains the 94-foot, full-scale model of a blue whale. Other museum treasures include the Star of India, the world's largest blue sapphire; a 34-ton section of the Cape York meteorite as old as the sun and its planets; and a 63-foot-long Haida war canoe.

Lying adjacent to the museum is a structure that looks like a giant sphere suspended within a massive glass cube—the Rose Center for Earth and Space, featuring the new Hayden Planetarium. The original planetarium, built in the 1930s, served as the backdrop in a scene from the Woody Allen film *Manhattan*. The planetarium was torn down in 1997 and reopened in 2000; today visitors flock to see its 3-D shows depicting the universe.

Above: The American Museum of Natural History appears stately in this photo from the early 1900s. Since its inception, the museum has been at the forefront of science by expanding its collections and sponsoring scientific expeditions.
Right: The top half of the Hayden Planetarium houses the Star Theater, while the bottom half features the Big Bang Theater.

CENTRAL PARK

In 1859, Central Park, the first landscaped public park in the United States, opened its vast expanses of greenery, fountains, bridges, and pathways to New York City's residents. At the time, there were wealthy New Yorkers who owned spacious mansions, but there were many more city dwellers who lived in cramped tenement apartments. The park provided a quiet escape from crowded city life.

Central Park was designed in 1857 by American landscape designer Frederick Law Olmsted and English architect Calvert Vaux, the winners of the first landscape design contest in the United States. Although their "Greensward Plan" called for manicured landscapes, the original area was filled with swamps and rocky outcroppings. Many groups of people also lived in or near the area, such as poor German immigrants, Irish pork farmers, and African Americans in a settlement called Seneca Village. Unfortunately, they were all displaced when park construction began.

More than 20,000 workers toiled to transform the space. Boulders were blasted with gunpowder, and poor soil was replaced with massive amounts of fertile topsoil from New Jersey. Horse-drawn carts carried more than 10 million cartloads of material to and from the area. And talk about pastoral: Sheep grazed on the appropriately named Sheep Meadow until 1934, when they were moved upstate.

Despite its initial ideals, over time the park fell into disrepair. By the 1970s, trampled lawns, graffiti, and crime plagued the space. In 1980, the Central Park Conservancy was founded, and the park was eventually restored to its former glory.

Today, with lakes, quaint bridges, and the fairy-tale Belvedere Castle, the park continues to draw millions of visitors to its 843 acres from West 59th to West 110th streets. The park also plays host to a number of free events, including the Shakespeare in the Park series, talks by speakers such as the Dalai Lama, and concerts featuring a vast variety of music genres and performers.

Above: In 1862, this squatter's shack lay just outside of Central Park. Dozens of similar shacks were razed when Central Park was built. In the distance on the right, the Cop Cot rustic shelter is visible, which still stands in Central Park. *Right:* Ice skaters glide along the 72nd Street Lake in Central Park in 1894. Ice skating remains a park tradition to this day.

Left: Central Park's expanses sit against a backdrop of the New York City skyline. *Below:* An early plan, circa 1857, describes "The Central Park As It Will Be When Laid Out."

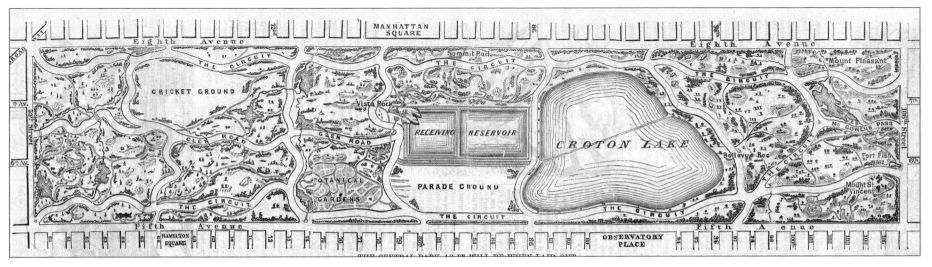

Beloved Characters

Well-known characters from Lewis Carroll's *Alice's Adventures in Wonderland* enchant visitors young and old on 75th Street just north of Conservatory Water. A statue of Hans Christian Andersen stands one block away, and Balto, a real-life heroic dog, is immortalized in a bronze statue on East 67th Street near the East Drive.

Visitors to Central Park can enjoy both nature and historic architecture in one setting. Here, skyscrapers cast a reflection on a Central Park South pond. The building in the forefront on the right is the Plaza Hotel, a U.S. National Landmark.

Dog walkers are a common sight in Central Park's lush interior. There's even an organization of dog owners who use the park, called Central Park Paws. The group puts out a newsletter called *The Central Barker*.

Bethesda Fountain

Of the 51 sculptures in Central Park, Bethesda Fountain contains the only one included in the park's original design. The other 50 works of art were donated to the space. The fountain was sculpted by Emma Stebbins, the first woman to be commissioned for such a work of art in NYC. Stebbins was inspired by a biblical passage from the Gospel of St. John that describes a pool in Jerusalem called Bethesda, said to have healing waters. In the fountain, an angel cradles a lily in her hand—a symbol of purity. The four surrounding figures represent peace, health, purity, and temperance.

THE METROPOLITAN MUSEUM OF ART

The two million-square-foot Metropolitan Museum of Art encompasses some of the world's greatest artistic treasures, spanning from ancient times to the present day. Founded in 1870 by a group of American artists and financiers, the museum moved to several locations before settling in its permanent home on 5th Avenue between 80th and 84th streets.

In 2007, the museum unveiled its New Greek and Roman Galleries, featuring more than 6,000 artistic treasures. The focal point is designed to resemble a Roman villa's colonnaded garden. In fact, two rooms from actual Roman villas buried when Vesuvius erupted in A.D. 79 were unearthed, restored, and brought to the Metropolitan.

The American wing of the museum includes a portrait of George Washington by Gilbert Stuart and Emanuel Leutze's enormous and iconic painting *Washington Crossing the Delaware,* which nearly covers an entire wall. The European collection's paintings and sculptures of Degas's ballerinas have long enchanted visitors. Scores of Van Gogh artwork are on display, such as his Cypress series, depicting tall, twisting trees; *Self Portrait with Hat* and *Irises* are also on display. Claude Monet's works can also be found gracing the museum's walls, including his color-flecked *Haystacks, Rouen Cathedral,* and *Bridge over a Pond of Water Lilies.*

In the musical instruments collection, traditional bagpipes, harpsichords, and lutes are on display alongside a Cristofori piano from 1720, one of the first pianos ever built. The museum has also hosted a number of special exhibitions, including such highlights as art from China's Ming Dynasty, armor from Tibet, and selections from the Modern Design collection.

Light floods through the museum's Temple of Dendur wing in 1996. The temple once sat on a hillside facing the Nile in Nubia (now Sudan) circa 15 B.C.

Medieval Marvel

The Cloisters Museum & Gardens is the museum's branch in Fort Tryon Park in northern Manhattan. Devoted to medieval European art and architecture, the museum's serene setting features the curved arches and columns of a 12th-century European cloister and a medieval garden with fragrant flowers and medicinal plants.

Left: The soaring ceilings of the Metropolitan Museum of Art's lobby create an impressive introduction to the building.

MUSEUM MILE

On 5th Avenue, from 82nd Street to 105th, lies an enclave of cultural and artistic treasures dubbed the Museum Mile. Some of the nine museums are housed in the former mansions of wealthy industrialists, such as the Cooper-Hewitt National Design Museum, which was once Andrew Carnegie's palatial residence. The mansion became a museum in 1976; since then it has housed collections of historic and modern design. There visitors can view drawings by artistic luminaries such as Winslow Homer and Frederic Church; it also has a vast textile collection including handcrafted European lace and silk dating as far back as the 13th century.

The stately Neue Galerie New York dates from 1914, and it was designed by Carrère & Hastings, the architects of the New York Public Library. Once occupied by Mrs. Cornelius Vanderbilt III, the building was renovated and transformed in 2001 into a museum featuring early 20th-century German and Austrian art. The Neue collection includes works from Egon Schiele and Oscar Kokoschka, as well as the magnificent Gustav Klimt painting *Adele Bloch-Bauer*, a portrait rendered in Klimt's characteristic detailed shapes and golden tones.

Just three blocks away is the Solomon R. Guggenheim Museum, a modernistic, spiral building designed by Frank Lloyd Wright in 1959. Dedicated to artwork from the late 19th century to the present, the museum's swirling walls have presented an eclectic array of styles and mediums.

The Jewish Museum is dedicated to showcasing the art and history of 4,000 years of Jewish culture. Founded in a library in 1904, the museum moved to its current building in 1947, after Frieda Schiff Warburg, widow of philanthropist Felix Warburg, generously donated the family's mansion on 5th Avenue to serve as the museum's permanent home.

Every year, on the second Tuesday in June, the Museum Mile Festival closes off a large section of 5th Avenue to cars, and there is no charge to enter the museums that line the block.

Above: Covering an entire city block, the Carnegie mansion's cost was estimated at $1 million—an extravagant amount at a time when few could afford that price. Here, the mansion is pictured in 1946. *Right:* Huge figures of the three Magi are marched down 5th Avenue at El Museo del Barrio in 1997. Especially popular in Spanish-speaking countries, Three King's Day is celebrated each January 6.

The Jewish Museum

The Jewish Museum on 5th Avenue's Museum Mile has been expanded numerous times, including the addition of a sculpture court in 1959. Inside the museum, visitors can find exhibitions on the history of Jewish culture, from important artwork and artifacts to dialogues on social politics.

Architect Frank Lloyd Wright used an inverted ziggurat, a winding pyramidal temple native to Babylonia, as the inspiration for the Guggenheim's layout. Visitors take an elevator to the top floor, then wind their way through the building's spiral ramps, enjoying artwork on the walls at every turn.

Above: Hundreds of people, such as this sculptor in 1909, contributed to the cathedral's construction. *Left:* St. John the Divine as it looked in 1910.

CATHEDRAL OF ST. JOHN THE DIVINE

One of New York's largest houses of worship, the Cathedral of St. John the Divine dates back to 1892, but setbacks in construction, including World War II and a raging fire, led some New Yorkers to dub the building "St. John the Unfinished."

The eastern part of the massive granite-faced cathedral was designed by the architectural firm of Heins & LaFarge, which employed the characteristic curves of the Romanesque style. After Heins's death in 1907, architect Ralph Adams Cram was hired to complete the cathedral, working in the Gothic style on the western flank.

Today, soaring stained-glass windows flood the cathedral with light, and a huge rose window graces the façade. Peacocks strut through the surrounding gardens. The great bronze doors—weighing three tons each—depict biblical scenes from the Creation to the Apocalypse. In fact, the same French foundry that cast the Statue of Liberty worked on St. John's doors, which are only opened on special occasions, such as the visits of the Dalai Lama and Nelson Mandela and at Easter, the peak of the liturgical year.

On the first Sunday in October, the annual feast day of St. Francis of Assisi,

patron saint of animals, is celebrated at St. John's. Many animals, including an elephant, a camel, and countless pet dogs, cats, and birds have passed through the doors to receive the bishop's blessing on that day.

In 2001, a fire broke out in the church gift shop. When firefighters arrived, they were asked to leave the precious stained-glass windows intact. As a result, soot filled the cathedral; restoration took years to complete. The great 8,000-pipe organ suffered heavy smoke damage and was silent until late 2008, when it once again filled the cathedral with sacred music.

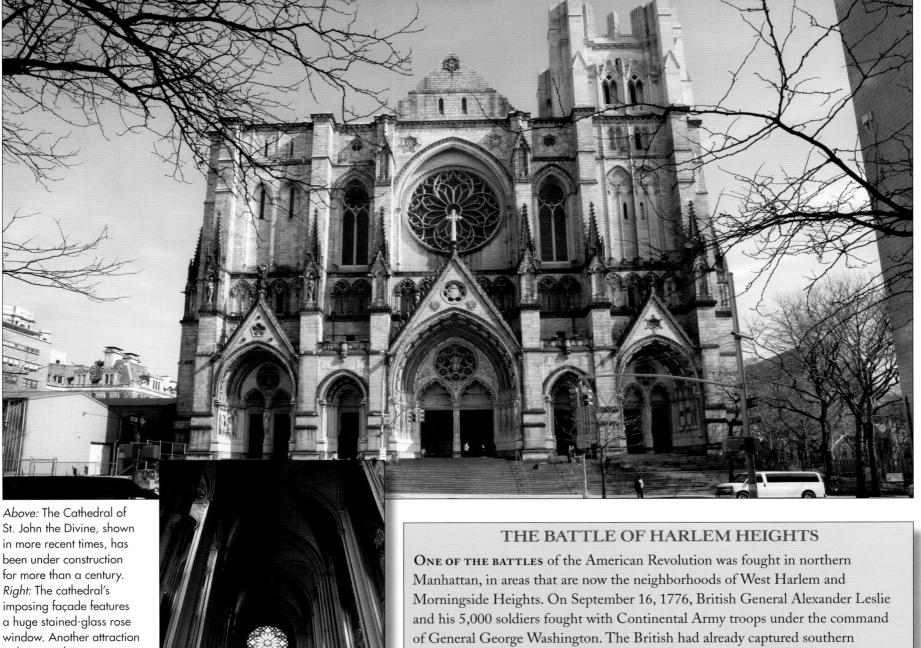

Above: The Cathedral of St. John the Divine, shown in more recent times, has been under construction for more than a century.
Right: The cathedral's imposing façade features a huge stained-glass rose window. Another attraction is the central entrance to the cathedral, the Portal of Paradise, which shows St. John and 32 biblical characters carved in stone.

THE BATTLE OF HARLEM HEIGHTS

ONE OF THE BATTLES of the American Revolution was fought in northern Manhattan, in areas that are now the neighborhoods of West Harlem and Morningside Heights. On September 16, 1776, British General Alexander Leslie and his 5,000 soldiers fought with Continental Army troops under the command of General George Washington. The British had already captured southern Manhattan, so tension ran high among the American soldiers. The Continental Army knew it had to do everything it could to retain control of the northern part of the island. In the end, Washington's brilliant strategy led his troops to victory. Although they outnumbered their foes, the British soldiers realized that the Continental Army surrounded them on three sides, and they were forced to retreat. The battle itself was a minor one, but the victory boosted the morale of the American army and inspired them to continue their struggle against the British.

HARLEM

The Dutch settlement established in northern Manhattan in 1658 remained mostly farmland until the 1800s. By the turn of the century, parts of Harlem were lined with elegant row houses for the wealthy, including those designed on West 139th Street by McKim, Mead and White for an affluent white clientele. In the 1920s, the area was dubbed Strivers' Row, when residents included celebrities such as "Father of the Blues" W. C. Handy, Bill "Bojangles" Robinson, and Scott Joplin. Clubs and churches sprang up, and 125th Street became Harlem's central thoroughfare.

Jewish immigrants came to Harlem in the early 1900s, and Italians moved to East Harlem in the 1930s. Although some Italian Americans remain, as well as their church, Our Lady of Mount Carmel, the section is currently known as Spanish Harlem because of its large Latino population. After subways were extended in Harlem, a surplus of new tenement houses led landlords to rent to African Americans. By 1930, about half of New York City's African Americans lived in the neighborhood.

Soon, Harlem became known for its legendary jazz scene, with the Apollo Theater hosting Count Basie, Duke Ellington, and other luminaries. The Cotton Club featured Cab Calloway's energetic orchestra, tap-dancing by the Nicholas Brothers, and eclectic vaudeville performances. An unfortunate sign of the times, the Cotton Club was restricted to a white audience, even though the entertainers were mostly African American.

In the 1920s and '30s, the neighborhood also played home to the Harlem Renaissance, a groundbreaking cultural movement of African American art, music, and literature. In 1926, writers such as Wallace Thurman, Langston Hughes, and Zora Neale Hurston published *Fire!!*, a literary magazine that epitomized the soul of the Harlem Renaissance.

Since the 1990s, the area has enjoyed a renewal of its former glory. New, upscale condominiums and renovations of historic brownstone houses have brought an economic revival to Harlem.

Above: The Abyssinian Baptist Church is seen in its current location in this photo from 1923. Before moving to Harlem, the church had several previous locations.

The Abyssinian Baptist Church fills with worshippers during a Sunday morning service in 2005. Established in the early 1800s, the church was named by Ethiopian settlers in New York for the ancient name of their country: Abyssinia. The present-day church is renowned, among other things, for its talented gospel choir.

Left: Cab Calloway leads his orchestra for couples celebrating New Year's Eve 1937 at the Cotton Club.

Historic buildings line Lenox Avenue in Harlem. On the left, St. Martin's Episcopal Church, designed by William A. Potter, soars above its surroundings. Nearly destroyed by two fires, the Romanesque Revival–style church was rebuilt and stands today. During the late 1940s, a 42-bell carillon was installed in the church tower. The carillon is one of the largest in NYC, second only to Riverside Church.

A POET IN HARLEM

IN THE 1920S, a cultural movement of African American literature, music, and art developed in Harlem, known as the Harlem Renaissance.

Writer Langston Hughes emerged as one of the central literary figures of that time. Born in Missouri in 1902, Hughes later moved to Harlem, although he also lived for a time in Mexico and France, where he was part of the black expatriate community.

Hughes was a prolific writer, penning poetry, short stories, novels, and more, describing the African American experience in a way many had never heard before. His collections of poetry include *Shakespeare in Harlem* and *One-Way Ticket,* and he was known for his play *Mulatto.*

After his death in 1967, Hughes's body was cremated, and his ashes now rest under a floor medallion near the Langston Hughes Auditorium in Harlem's Arturo Alfonso Schomburg Center for Research in Black Culture. Inscribed in the tile is a line from one of his poems, reading, "My soul has grown deep like the rivers."

Originally built as a burlesque house in 1914, the Apollo Theater is a historic landmark in Harlem. The venue (seen here in 1922) became famous for its Amateur Nite at the Apollo, where many entertainers, including Billie Holiday and Jimi Hendrix, got their starts.

It's Showtime

The Apollo Theater has become one of the most famous theaters for African American performers, including Louis Armstrong, Sarah Vaughn, Bessie Smith, Sam Cooke, Aretha Franklin, and Diana Ross. James Brown made his debut at the Apollo in 1956. In 2006, when the legendary soul singer died of heart failure, his body was placed in an open coffin for public viewing within the venue. His body was transported down the streets of Harlem to the theater in a horse-drawn carriage.

RANDALL'S ISLAND

In 1637, Dutch governor Wouter Van Twiller purchased a small island in the East River from the Native Americans. As the years rolled by, the land was used for many things, including farming and later as a station for British soldiers. Because of its separation from northern Manhattan and Queens, the land also served as a home for quarantined smallpox victims. In the late 1790s, Jonathan Randall bought the island, and his descendants sold it to New York City some 50 years later.

On Randall's Island, the city established a burial ground for the indigent, a rest home for veterans of the Civil War, a homeopathic hospital, and other health facilities. In 1933, the institutions were closed, and the island became home to a park and recreational facilities. Since the 1930s, Randall's Island has also been connected to Wards Island to the south, after the city ordered a body of water known as Little Hell Gate to be filled in.

With the 1936 opening of the Triborough Bridge (renamed the Robert F. Kennedy Bridge in 2008), the island was made more accessible. Downing Stadium was built there, and in the stadium's plaza, a bronze statue, *The Discus Thrower* by Greek sculptor Kostas Dimitriadis, stood as the symbol of the island. Track phenom Jesse Owens emerged as the winner of the 100-yard dash in the 1936 Olympic Trials in Downing Stadium. Various other sports celebrities have also played there, including soccer great Pele. Golf champion Tiger Woods ran a children's golf clinic in the stadium in 1996.

After Downing Stadium was demolished in 2002, the new Icahn Stadium opened three years later. In 1997, Randall's Island Golf Center opened on 25 acres, where golfers can enjoy a day on the green.

On July 12, 1936, Jesse Owens races past other runners to win the 100-yard dash at the final Olympic track and field tryouts on Randall's Island. Owens went on to win four gold medals at the Berlin Olympics that year.

Randall's Island, seen in the foreground, sits across the East River from Manhattan's skyline.

Queens
THE MELTING POT

In an already international city, Queens remains one of the most diverse counties in the entire nation. Here you'll find the largest population of East Indians outside of their mother country, as well as Jewish, Korean, Italian, Greek, Irish, Latino, and other ethnic communities. Islamic mosques, Hindu temples, Catholic and Protestant churches, Jewish synagogues, and other varied houses of worship all share the expanses of Queens.

The largest in area of the five boroughs, Queens sprawls over 100 square miles, encompassing a space almost as large as the Bronx, Manhattan, and Staten Island combined. Although Queens is physically located on the western flank of fish-shaped Long Island, it is politically a part of New York City. Two of the major NYC airports, La Guardia Airport and John F. Kennedy International Airport, call this vibrant area home.

A BOROUGH IS BORN
The first inhabitants of Queens were the Paleo-Indians, and later, the Lenape tribe. Until the arrival of the Dutch in 1635, these native peoples enjoyed the bounties of the region's rolling hills and fish-filled waterways. Even from its colonial beginnings, Queens was an area of diverse ethnicities. Although the region was part of the Dutch-ruled New Netherland territory in its early days, both Dutch and English settlers came to coexist there. Small towns such as Newtown (present-day Elmhurst), Vlissingen (present-day Flushing), and Maspeth sprang up in the 1600s.

In 1683, Queens County was formed. It was three times its current size because it originally included all of Nassau County and parts of Suffolk County, which are now politically parts of Long Island. Queens County's name is said to have honored Catherine of Braganza, the Portuguese-born wife of Charles II, king of England.

The borough of Queens officially came into existence on January 1, 1898, when the New York State Legislature created

In this 1920 photo taken during the days of Prohibition, dozens of men staged a mock funeral for the last bottle of liquor in a bar in Astoria, Queens.

Opposite: A view of the old Shea Stadium, which was built near the site of the 1964–65 World's Fair. Here, the New York Mets play during their 1966 season.

the Greater City of New York, merging the boroughs of Manhattan, Brooklyn, the Bronx, Staten Island, and Queens into one metropolis. In 1899, however, a large part of what was then Eastern Queens seceded and became Nassau County in Long Island. For most of the 18th and 19th centuries, Queens was a quiet agricultural area. When a ferry began crossing the East River from Manhattan to Astoria in Queens, the borough slowly grew.

In the mid-1800s, a wave of Irish and German immigrants arrived in New York; some found work in the breweries and factories of a rapidly industrialized Queens County. In 1872, the Steinway Piano Factory moved from Manhattan to its present location in Queens. In addition to the factory, Steinway also provided housing for employees, a park, and a post office.

STEADY GROWTH
As bridges and tunnels were built, it became easier for people to reside in Queens and still be within a short ride of their jobs in Manhattan. In 1915, when the Number 7 subway line was built throughout parts of Queens as an extension to the established subway system, this too fueled the borough's population growth.

At first, the Great Depression of the 1930s caused a slowdown of the borough's boom, but the opening of the Whitestone Bridge and Robert F. Kennedy (formerly the Triborough) Bridge reversed the downward trend. Things perked up considerably after the end of World War II, as major developments—including the Idlewild Airport (now John F. Kennedy International Airport), major highways such as the Long Island Expressway, and the growth of high-rise apartment buildings—increased the flow of immigrants to the area.

QUEENS TODAY
Sitcoms such as *All in the Family* and *The King of Queens* have painted a picture of tightly spaced row houses and high traffic. While parts of Queens are admittedly densely populated, the borough also features a suburban atmosphere. Here, huge expanses of both natural and manicured greenery sprawl across the otherwise urban landscape, often surrounded by water in this city of islands. The Jamaica Bay Wildlife Refuge, near John F. Kennedy International Airport in the southwest section of Queens, is the sole wildlife refuge in the entire national park system. The area's more than 9,000 acres of salt marsh and ponds provide shelter for fish, butterflies, small mammals, and more than 300 species of birds.

The region has also seen its share of glamour: Flushing Meadows Park provided the backdrop for two world's fairs.

The Louis Armstrong House Museum in Corona honors the memory of the late entertainer and gives visitors an intimate look at the home where Armstrong and his wife lived for many years.

The 1939–40 New York World's Fair transformed what was once the unsavory Corona Dump into an international gathering place, with the distinctive sights of the Trylon, Perisphere, and Helicline structures looming above the fairgrounds.

Twenty-four years after the first fair closed, the 1964–65 New York World's Fair, broadcasting a theme of "Peace Through Understanding," once again brought an international flair to Queens.

Visitors could find a re-created medieval Belgian Village, where they savored Belgian waffles with strawberries and cream; and the Vatican pavilion, which displayed the Michelangelo masterpiece *Pietà*. In the Johnson's Wax Pavilion, visitors were transported up under an expansive egg-shape dome to see the award-winning film *To Be Alive*. The Unisphere, the New York Hall of Science, and the current Flushing Meadows Corona Park still stand as reminders of that World's Fair from long ago.

Sports continue to flourish in Queens; the borough is home to the USTA Billie Jean King National Tennis Center, which hosts the annual U.S. Open competitions. Baseball has always played a large role in Queens. From Shea Stadium's opening in 1964 until it was dismantled section by section in 2008, the ballpark was the home of the New York Mets baseball team. In 2009, the Mets opened the season in their new home, Citi Field, with its roomy seats and wide, unobstructed concourses.

Visitors stroll by the New York Hall of Science's North Wing. Opened in 2004, the expansive addition is dedicated to informing and entertaining young visitors with exhibits on math, art, space, and technology.

THE NOGUCHI MUSEUM

The Noguchi Museum in Long Island City, Queens, lies one block from the East River, which separates Queens from Manhattan. Founded by artist and landscape architect Isamu Noguchi, the museum opened in 1985. Once an industrial building, the museum now features 13 galleries highlighting the artist's works. Visitors can view Noguchi's various mediums, ranging from sculptures crafted from metal, clay, and stone, to models for his garden and public project designs. It also includes models of his stage sets for dance performances and his Akari Light Sculptures.

Born in 1904 in Los Angeles to an American mother and a Japanese father, Noguchi spent his early years in Japan and then later lived in the United States. Just out of high school, he apprenticed with sculptor Gutzon Borglum, renowned for his sculptures of the U.S. presidents at Mount Rushmore. After winning a Guggenheim Fellowship, Noguchi traveled to Paris, where he studied with the acclaimed Romanian sculptor Constantin Brancusi. In 1939, his *Chassis Fountain* sculpture graced the Ford Motor Company's pavilion at the New York World's Fair. In 1955, he created sets and costumes for the Royal Shakespeare Company's production of *King Lear,* starring Sir John Gielgud.

In 1961, Noguchi set up a studio in a small building in Long Island City, then mostly an industrial area. Across the street was another building that later became his museum. Noguchi's career spanned over 60 years, and he continued to work until his death in 1988.

After a major renovation from 2002 to 2004 to stabilize the former photoengraving plant built in 1928, the museum currently houses an extensive permanent collection of Noguchi's works, including a gallery devoted to the artist's work in interior design.

Left: While famous for his open-air and abstract sculptures, Noguchi was also able to sculpt in a more traditional sense. Here he poses in 1926 with *Undine (Nadja),* his only full-figure sculpture that is still known to exist. *Below:* The surrounding garden at the museum displays some of Noguchi's basalt and granite sculptures. The sculpture in the foreground is called *The Illusion of the Fifth Stone.*

Above: Viewers take part in France Night at the park's annual summer Outdoor Cinema festival.
Left: The Socrates Sculpture Park hosts many events and exhibits, including this EAF05: 2005 Emerging Artist Fellowship Exhibition.

SOCRATES SCULPTURE PARK

Located in Long Island City, adjoining the waterfront where the East River and the Harlem River converge, Socrates Sculpture Park is both an outdoor museum and a public park. It was named for the Greek philosopher Socrates, with a nod to the residents of nearby Astoria, NYC's largest Greek community.

Once an abandoned landfill and illegal dumping ground filled with garbage and graffiti, a coalition of artists and local residents led by sculptor Mark di Suvero worked to save the space. In 1986, they succeeded, and the 4.5-acre area was transformed from an eyesore into a verdant expanse that neighborhood residents regard with pride. In 1993, Socrates Sculpture Park became part of the NYC Parks Department.

The park's mission is to provide emerging artists with a place to both create and exhibit their large-scale artwork. Sculptors work on their projects in an open-air studio, allowing visitors an opportunity to view the progress of sculptures as they are created. After completion, the sculptures are put on display against the backdrop of the Manhattan skyline in the distance. Admission to the park is free, and it is open every day, year-round.

The park hosts many special events, including an annual Halloween Harvest Festival with live music, games, and a treat for dog-lovers: the Canine Costume Contest. Each summer, the park features its free weekly Festival of International Film, Music, Dance and Food, in collaboration with the Museum of the Moving Image and Partnership for Parks. In the past, movies on the outdoor screen have included films from Greece, Mexico, South Korea, France, and Italy. Samples of ethnic food from local restaurants are also served.

MUSEUM OF THE MOVING IMAGE

It's fitting that the Museum of the Moving Image is located in Astoria, the town that played home to the movie industry's earliest days in the 1920s. Today, the museum houses the world's largest collection of artifacts related to film, television, and more. With 130,000 objects and counting, the museum's collection features still photographs, video and computer games, historical movie theater furnishings, costumes, fan magazines, toys, and other memorabilia, all portraying the fascinating history of the technology and artistic creations of moving images.

Opened in 1988 in a renovated industrial building, the facility's core exhibition, *Behind the Screen,* chronicles the development of the illusion of movement from early devices like an 1880 "Magic Lantern" that projected images onto a screen to advanced computer editing demonstrations. The museum even features prosthetics from classic films such as *The Godfather, The Exorcist,* and the original *Star Wars.* The exhibit also has historic action figures, posters, and even lunch boxes featuring memorable film and TV characters such as Howdy Doody.

Changing temporary exhibits in the past have included *Star Trek: 40 Years of Fandom, Gumby and the Art of Stop-Motion Animation,* and *Tim Burton Drawings.* For three years, the museum exhibited the original set of *Seinfeld*'s Monk's Café, where the characters Jerry, George, Elaine, and Kramer once sat in a booth and complained about life in the big city and relationships gone awry. Ongoing film screenings have included visits from film luminaries such as Sidney Lumet, Ang Lee, Marisa Tomei, Danny Glover, and Wong Kar-Wai.

In February 2008, the museum embarked on an expansion to double its size. Slated to open in 2010, the renovated museum will include a new theater for screenings of both contemporary and classic films, expanded galleries, and a new education center to enlighten visitors about the world of film.

Ready . . . Action!

The Astoria Studio (above) stands at the corner of 35th Avenue and 35th Street, as photographed in 1925. At the time, the studio held numerous stages; sometimes up to six feature films would be in production at once. The Museum of the Moving Image's collection of vintage cameras includes this Akeley 35mm "Pancake" motion picture camera from 1918 (left). Carl Akeley, then a curator at the American Museum of Natural History and an explorer and inventor, designed the hand-cranked camera to film his field expeditions in Africa.

QUEENS AND THE SILVER SCREEN

THE MOVIE INDUSTRY'S EARLY DAYS were important ones for the borough. In 1920, the Kaufman Astoria Studios opened in Queens. The studio was the home of Paramount Pictures, where classic films were made starring big-screen luminaries such as Rudolph Valentino, W. C. Fields, Gloria Swanson, and Lillian Gish. Productions at Kaufman included the talking film debuts of stars such as Edward G. Robinson and Claudette Colbert. The daffy Marx Brothers also made their transition from Broadway to the silver screen at the studio.

After the movie industry left New York City for the sunny skies of California, Kaufman Astoria Studios ceased producing films. But in 1976, the studio was declared a National Historic Landmark, and it underwent a renaissance when it reopened in 1977. Today, Kaufman encompasses a whole complex of facilities, including the largest stage on the East Coast and a music-recording studio.

Above: The Museum of the Moving Image screens classic films daily in its Tut's Fever Movie Palace, with its kitschy Egyptian statues and decorations. *Right:* The expanded museum will reopen in 2010 with twice as much space and a three-story addition, as pictured here.

THE LOUIS ARMSTRONG HOUSE MUSEUM

Louis "Satchmo" Armstrong blazed a trail for jazz musicians, playing the cornet and trumpet and singing in his characteristic raspy voice. Duke Ellington called him "the epitome of jazz." A longtime resident of Corona, Queens, Armstrong and his wife, Lucille, lived in a small house, which became a museum after his death.

Against all odds, Armstrong rose to success. Born into poverty in 1901 in a New Orleans section dubbed "the Battlefield," he was put into a home for delinquents when he was 11. There he learned to play the cornet and continued developing his skills. Armstrong sang, played, and composed for the next 50 years; many of his renditions of classic standards live on, including "What a Wonderful World" and "Hello, Dolly."

Armstrong traveled extensively, entertaining audiences around the world. In 1943, embarking on a musical tour, he asked Lucille to purchase a house while he was away. Despite the entertainer's huge earnings, Lucille chose a modest residence on 107th Street, where they lived for the rest of their lives.

A National Historic Landmark since 1976, the Louis Armstrong House Museum opened in 2003. Visitors experience the house much as it was when the Armstrongs lived there. Lucille's love of color and rich décor shows throughout, as well as her ingenuity: Mirrors on the door and every wall of a small bathroom make the space appear larger. Satchmo's private office still contains his original desk and chair. Visitors can also view the master bedroom, where Armstrong passed away in his sleep in 1971.

Besides ongoing house tours, every February Black History Month programs include lectures about the jazz celebrity. Each July, the museum also sponsors a free outdoor jazz concert and block party.

Above: Inside the Louis Armstrong House, the entertainer's private study remains much the same as he left it. On the wall at left is a painting of Armstrong, created for him by singer Tony Bennett.

Despite his celebrity status, Louis Armstrong frequently entertained neighborhood children and even allowed them to try out his instruments.

NEW YORK HALL OF SCIENCE

Originally built for the 1964–65 New York World's Fair, the New York Hall of Science is one of a handful of buildings that remained open after the fair closed. The hands-on science and technology center entertains while educating visitors with more than 400 interactive exhibits exploring the worlds of biology, chemistry, genetics, and more. In 2004, the new 55,000-square-foot North Wing doubled the size of the already expansive museum.

The Realm of the Atom allows visitors to examine the world's first 3-D, dynamic model of an atom. Relying on the theories of quantum physics pioneers Niels Bohr, Werner Heisenberg, and Erwin Schrodinger, the model of a hydrogen atom was built at a magnification of one billion times the original.

The museum's outdoor Rocket Park is home to icons of the early U.S. space program. An original *Atlas* booster stands tall, alongside a replica of a *Mercury* capsule and an original *Titan II* booster. The park also features an interactive replica of the *Friendship 7 Mercury* capsule, where visitors can climb aboard for an up-close experience of the astronauts' quarters. Indoors at the museum, the first *Mercury* capsule ever created and flown is on display.

The museum also features an outdoor Science Playground, the largest such playground in the Western hemisphere. Here, the principles of physics come alive to children through physical activities like coasting down a slide or climbing a giant spider web.

Below: A postcard from the 1964–65 New York World's Fair shows the pavilion's three main structures, including a circular theater known as the "Tent of Tomorrow." The structures remain but are in poor condition.

Making Science Fun

Above, students peek inside a large model of the brain at the New York Hall of Science's exhibit, *Brain: The World Inside Your Head.* The New York Hall of Science's Great Hall (right photo, center) was built for the 1964–65 New York World's Fair. Its wavy design features thousands of multicolored pieces of glass embedded inside tall concrete walls.

In this aerial view of the 1964–65 New York World's Fair, the Unisphere is seen with jets of water shooting up from its surrounding fountains. The fair's broad pedestrian streets are flanked with flags from various nations.

THE UNISPHERE

The symbol of the 1964–65 New York World's Fair, the gleaming Unisphere, still stands in Flushing Meadows Corona Park where it was once the centerpiece of the fairgrounds. The world's largest representation of the earth, the stainless steel structure stands 140 feet high—as tall as a 12-story building—and measures 120 feet in diameter.

The fair's theme was "Peace Through Understanding." Robert Moses, the president of the World's Fair Corporation at the time, said of the Unisphere, "We looked high and low for a challenging symbol.... It had to reflect the interdependence of man on the planet Earth, and it had to emphasize man's achievements and aspirations."

Designed by Gilmore Clark, the gigantic, 700,000-ton globe was a gift from U.S. Steel, the company that built the Empire State Building. Their American Bridge Division created the sphere in sections in Harrisburg, Pennsylvania, following contour maps made by the U.S. Army Corps of Engineers. The continents have exaggerated mountains and valleys so they can easily be seen from near and far. Circling the globe are three rings, symbolizing satellites encircling the earth.

An open sphere resting on a 70-ton pedestal base in the center of a fountain, the Unisphere was constructed to withstand gale-force winds and the rain and heavy snows that occur in New York City. From the very start, it was meant as a permanent fixture in the park.

Today, with the World's Fair long gone, the Unisphere's glittering metal endures and continues to delight visitors. Even drivers on the Grand Central Parkway, the Long Island Expressway, and the Van Wyck Expressway can enjoy the view of the iconic sphere that has come to symbolize the borough of Queens.

Above: The setting sun casts a warm glow over the gleaming, curved metal of the Unisphere.
Left: A poster of the World's Fair, featuring the Unisphere. The world's largest representation of our planet has also become the unofficial symbol for the borough of Queens.

QUEENS MUSEUM OF ART

Housed in the only surviving building from the 1939 New York World's Fair, the present-day Queens Museum of Art boasts a permanent collection including an archive of more than 6,000 photographs, films, and other memorabilia of both the 1939–40 and the 1964–65 New York World's fairs. Past exhibits have included *Erasing Borders: Indian Artists in the American Diaspora* and *Down the Garden Path: The Artist's Garden After Modernism.*

The highlight of the museum is the *Panorama of the City of New York.* Originally created for the 1964–65 New York World's Fair, the detailed architectural model features a representation of every building constructed before 1992, when it was renovated. The vast 3-D model measures more than 9,000 square feet and includes 895,000 structures in each of the five boroughs, replete with miniature trees and bodies of water. Architectural model makers Raymond Lester Associates created the vast panorama, assigning a team of 100 workers to the project, which was completed in three years.

The Queens Museum of Art is also the proud owner of the Neustadt Collection of Tiffany Art, an impressive assortment of the ornate stained-glass lamps created by Louis Comfort Tiffany and his studio. Among the stunning objects in this collection are a glass globe adorned with pond lilies, a hanging lampshade with graceful decorations of red and pink peonies, and a dragonfly-bedecked library lamp. Floor lamps, hanging shades, and chandeliers by the famous stained-glass artist are in the collection, as well as large, leaded-glass windows.

In 2009, the museum began a one-year expansion, which doubled its current size to 100,000 square feet. Originally housed in the north side of the former World's Fair building, the expansion extended the Queens Museum of Art to the entire building.

Opposite: Students peer over the guardrail to view the sprawling *Panorama of the City of New York.* Parts of Brooklyn and Queens are seen at left, and Manhattan is represented on the right. A scale-model Staten Island is seen in the distance.

Right: The Trylon and Perisphere (at left) tower over the Grand Central Parkway at the 1939–40 New York World's Fair. Construction started on the parkway in 1931; it was finished in 1936, in plenty of time for motorists heading to the World's Fair. *Far right:* A poster of the 1939–40 New York World's Fair features its two symbols, the Trylon and Perisphere.

SPORTS IN QUEENS

Queens has long hosted sporting events ranging from tennis to the all-American pastime, baseball. In Flushing Meadows Corona Park, the USTA Billie Jean King National Tennis Center, named for the champion tennis player, opened in 1978. It has since been the site of the annual U.S. Open tennis tournament every summer. The event is the culmination of the Grand Slam Tournament. Located directly across from the former Shea Stadium, the tennis center features 22 courts, with an additional 11 courts in an adjacent park.

The center's main venue is the 22,000-seat Arthur Ashe Stadium, named for the acclaimed tennis player who was the first African American to win a Grand Slam event. Second in size, the center's older venue is the Louis Armstrong Stadium, which was named after the jazz musician who lived nearby.

From Billie Jean King to Steffi Graf, from Maria Sharapova to Venus and Serena Williams, the winners of the women's singles events have played here. Men's singles champions who have graced the center's courts include John McEnroe, Pete Sampras, and Roger Federer.

Another Queens sports icon, the former Shea Stadium opened in 1964. Over the years, the stadium hosted both baseball and football games. New York Jets great Joe Namath described the "strong winds" and "the brutal cold" of the stadium, but added that it gave his team "a great home-field advantage." Shea was also the venue for memorable concerts with musicians such as the Beatles and The Clash. For its final concerts in July 2008, Shea featured musicians Billy Joel, Tony Bennett, Aerosmith's Steven Tyler, and The Who's Roger Daltrey. The stadium closed in September 2008.

In 2009, the newly built Citi Field opened adjacent to the former Shea Stadium. The Mets' new ballpark features room for 45,000 spectators and boasts more luxury suites, restaurants, and public elevators than its predecessor.

Tennis, Anyone?

A 25-year-old Arthur Ashe holds his trophy after winning the first U.S. Open at the West Side Tennis Club in Forest Hills, Queens, on September 9, 1968. His opponent, Tom Okker of the Netherlands, looks on. Below, Amelie Mauresmo of France competes against Mara Santangelo of Italy on September 3, 2006, during the U.S. Open Tennis competition at Armstrong Stadium.

Crowds cheer as the New York Mets play the Pittsburgh Pirates in their first game at the newly opened Shea Stadium on April 17, 1964.

At the old Shea Stadium, whenever the Mets scored a home run, the Home Run Apple—a big apple emblazoned with the Mets logo—popped out of a huge magic hat. The tradition began in 1980.

From Shea to Citi Field

The original, 55,601-seat Shea Stadium, seen here on the left in 2005, featured huge neon decorations of baseball players on the exterior. But it wasn't just the Mets' home turf—the New York Yankees also played at Shea from 1974 to 1975, while Yankee Stadium was being renovated. The Mets' third and newest home, Citi Field (below), opened in 2009. Gone are the days of 1960s-era construction costs. While Shea Stadium cost $28.5 million to build, the total project costs for Citi Field are estimated at more than $600 million.

ETHNIC NEIGHBORHOODS

One of the most ethnically diverse counties in the nation, Queens is home to a number of neighborhoods sporting an international flair. On the north side of the borough, across the East River from Manhattan, lies Astoria, which became a village in 1839 and was the site of cottages, churches, and mansions for the wealthy. Today, the neighborhood has many different ethnicities, including the largest Greek community outside of Athens and a sizeable Croatian community.

Astoria is also home to the Bohemian Hall & Beer Garden, the oldest (and only) remaining outdoor beer garden of the hundreds that once thrived in New York City. Its indoor restaurant serves hearty Czech meals such as chicken paprikash and roasted pork with sauerkraut and dumplings. But vegetarians needn't stay away—meatless pierogi and potato pancakes are also on the menu.

Once a Dutch settlement, today's Flushing features all things Asian. Harboring NYC's second-largest Chinatown, Flushing brims with Chinese herbal shops vending a multitude of varieties of ginseng and teahouses serving traditional types or those with tapioca "bubbles" inside. In addition, Korean, Vietnamese and Indian restaurants line the town's streets. A magnificent Hindu temple with an ornately sculpted façade dedicated to the elephant-headed god Ganesh also can be found in Flushing.

Once a planned community for the commuting middle class after the Number 7 subway connected Queens to Manhattan, Jackson Heights is now an enclave of Indian cuisine and culture. Lining 74th Street, sari shops, Indian jewelry boutiques, and a plethora of restaurants with savory curries greet visitors and residents. Tempting Indian sweet shops offer an array of sugary Indian desserts.

Intrepid swimmers dip and dive at the Astoria Pool in 1936. The base of the Hell Gate Bridge looms in the background.

Crowds flock to Loew's Triboro Theatre on Steinway Street, Astoria, on its opening day, February 21, 1931. The grand exterior was in Mayan Revival–style, and the expansive interior was palatial, seating over 3,000 people. Unfortunately, the theater was demolished in 1974.

Queens has its own Little India section in Jackson Heights. Visitors can buy everything from authentic Indian curries and sweets to CDs featuring *bhangra* music.

The Great Procession

In Astoria, Queens, the Miraculous Weeping Icon of St. Irene Chrysovalantou is paraded under the elevated subway tracks in 2003. St. Irene is the patron saint of peace and of those suffering from diseases. The icon is said to have healing powers and to have wept for one month in 1990, before and during the Persian Gulf War. In a much-publicized event in 1991, armed robbers stole the icon. Days later, they anonymously returned the holy painting in the mail—missing its frame and precious gems.

QUEENS: BIRTHPLACE OF RELIGIOUS FREEDOM

ALTHOUGH NOT WIDELY KNOWN, the document called the Flushing Remonstrance is considered by some to be a forerunner of the U.S. Constitution's insistence on the freedom of religion.

In 1657, residents from Vlissingen (present-day Flushing) wrote and signed a "remonstrance," a document protesting then Governor Peter Stuyvesant's restrictions on Quaker worship. Upon signing and sending the remonstrance to the government, some of the signers were jailed for a short time.

Subsequently, John Bowne (whose wife had converted to Quakerism) allowed his home to be used as a meeting place for their religious services. For his efforts, he was jailed for three months and sent to the Netherlands to await trial. While there, he spoke with representatives of the Dutch West India Company, who eventually agreed that Quakers should be allowed to practice their religion in the colony across the water.

Bowne returned to Vlissingen, and Stuyvesant was ordered to uphold religious tolerance. After the British took control of the colony, changing its name to New York, they continued to grant religious freedom. Bowne died in 1695, but good works continued in his name: In the 19th century, his house became a stop on the Underground Railroad for slaves seeking freedom. The Bowne House still stands today as a reminder of the roots of our nation's religious independence.

Brooklyn
FROM FARMLAND TO FABULOUS

Brooklyn, New York City's most populous borough, once stood proudly as its own city. In fact, at the start of the Civil War, Brooklyn was the third-largest city in the nation. If it were currently an independent city, it would still stand as the fourth-largest city in the United States. Today's Brooklyn is a sublime mix of stately, traditional architecture alongside modern buildings. Great expanses of greenery, such as that found in Prospect Park and Marine Park, intermingle with busy, densely populated avenues and diverse neighborhoods. While it no longer stands as a city on its own, Brooklyn is a distinctive NYC borough with impressive cultural offerings and a flavorful multiethnic population.

A FORESTED LANDSCAPE

The area that became modern-day Brooklyn was at one time a densely forested land, noted for its excellent hunting. It was also once filled with fertile expanses that produced thriving crops. In addition, the land featured ample wetlands and a fine harbor that offered a natural shelter against severe storms. Much like the rest of the region, the Paleo-Indians were the first inhabitants, followed by the Lenape, who established villages and flourished in this area until the arrival of European settlers and Dutch West India Company in the 1630s.

Opposite: At the time of its completion on May 24, 1883, the Brooklyn Bridge (seen here in 1895) was hailed as "The Eighth Wonder of the World."

In 1646, the town of Breukelen (named after a town of the same name in the Netherlands) was founded as part of the Dutch-held New Netherland territories. The area comprised six small farming towns, five of which were Dutch. The other town, Gravesend, was British, and it held the distinction of being the only colonial town to be founded by a woman, Lady Deborah Moody.

THE BATTLE OF BROOKLYN

Brooklyn also played a pivotal role during the American Revolution. In 1776, when General Howe led the British army in the

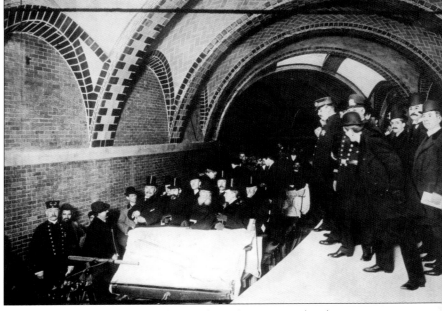

On October 27, 1904, New York City's first subway opened at the City Hall Station. Political dignitaries, financiers, and police officers are shown riding the cars.

Battle of Long Island (also known as the Battle of Brooklyn), he nearly destroyed General George Washington's army. But when Washington led his army across the East River, a dense fog allowed them to retreat unharmed to safety in Manhattan. Some historians think the revolution would have ended right then and there if the British could have stopped Washington's army from retreating.

LINKS TO MANHATTAN
Farmers in Brooklyn shuttled some of their produce to markets in Manhattan via ferry. A shipbuilding industry arose in 1801 with the opening of the Brooklyn Navy Yard, where vessels continued to be built until its closure in 1966. Among the famous ships built here were the *Monitor*—known for its distinction as the first ironclad ship in the United States as well as its use in the Civil War—and the battleship USS *Missouri*, a.k.a. "The Mighty Mo."

When the Brooklyn Bridge opened in 1883, the borough's population experienced a boom. Later, the construction of other bridges such as the Williamsburg Bridge (1903), the Manhattan Bridge (1909), and the Verrazano-Narrows Bridge (1964)—along with various subway lines and tunnels—added to Brooklyn's growth. In 1898, Brooklyn joined the other four boroughs and officially became part of New York City.

AN INTERNATIONAL BOROUGH
Brooklyn has always been a home for a variety of nationalities from around the world. In the mid-19th century, the first great wave of European immigrants—mostly Irish and German—arrived in the United States; many made Brooklyn their new home. Several decades later, from 1880 through the early 1900s, a second great wave of immigrants left their homes in Eastern and Southern Europe to settle in areas throughout the borough.

The trend continues even today: Of those moving to New York City from around the world and the United States, many settle in Brooklyn because rental prices are known to be a bit (but not much!) more affordable than in Manhattan. Brooklyn has also maintained its international atmosphere, including an extensive array of ethnic groups from far and wide, such as the Caribbean, Africa, Russia, the Mediterranean, and the Middle East.

GOOD GAME!
Brooklyn has always been a home for sports lovers—particularly baseball. The Brooklyn Dodgers baseball team, formed in 1883, played in several stadiums before moving to Ebbets Field in 1913. The team made history in 1947 when they added Jackie Robinson, the first African American major-league baseball player, to the roster. In 1957, the Dodgers moved to California where they became known as the Los Angeles Dodgers. Since 2001, the Brooklyn Cyclones (a minor-league team) have played at KeySpan Park in Coney Island.

But there's more to Brooklyn sports than just baseball. The Brooklyn Aces, a team in the Eastern Professional Hockey League, played its inaugural season in November 2008 in Brooklyn's 2,500-seat stadium in the Aviator Sports and Recreation complex. Soccer fans can also watch the Brooklyn Knights in this sports complex.

CULTURE AND ENTERTAINMENT
Today's Brooklyn offers residents and visitors a wealth of cultural opportunities, from the grandiose art-filled halls of the Brooklyn Museum to the eclectic DUMBO Arts Center. Readers can choose from a massive number of volumes in the Brooklyn Library, and

In recent years, the Brooklyn Museum has focused on revitalizing its exhibitions and redesigning its galleries.

visitors learn about the world of plants in the expansive Brooklyn Botanic Garden.

The Brooklyn Academy of Music, the Brooklyn Philharmonic, and the Mark Morris Dance Center offer a wide array of entertainment. The Brooklyn Children's Museum, the nation's first museum for youngsters, has entertained visitors since its opening in 1899. International dining is available throughout the borough, particularly on a wide stretch of Atlantic Avenue in Cobble Hill, where Middle Eastern shops and restaurants share the street with eateries featuring the cuisines of Spain, the Caribbean, Italy, Mexico, India, and more.

The Japanese Garden in the Brooklyn Botanic Garden is a serene sight. Japanese landscape designer Takeo Shiota created the space in 1915. It is considered his masterpiece.

THE BROOKLYN BRIDGE

Until the Brooklyn Bridge opened, the only way to cross the East River was by ferry. At the time, Brooklyn was its own city, and many residents commuted across the fast-moving river to work in Manhattan. One day in 1867, however, the river froze over, and the ferries were at a standstill. It was clear that something else was needed to unite the two cities.

John Roebling, a German immigrant and gifted engineer, suggested creating a suspension bridge to span the river. That year, he was appointed chief engineer of the project. In his preliminary report, he predicted the bridge would be "the great engineering work...of the age" as well as "a great work of art." His words proved true, but sadly, Roebling died in an accident before construction began in 1870.

Roebling's son, Washington, succeeded his father as chief engineer. The younger Roebling supervised as workers dug beneath the river, sheltered by huge wooden caissons. At the time, no one anticipated that ascending quickly from the high air pressure of the caissons would cause decompression sickness. Many workers experienced chest pains, and Roebling was nearly paralyzed from "caisson disease" (what we would now call the bends). His wife, Emily, carried his instructions to and from workers as he watched the construction through a spyglass from his sickbed in Brooklyn. He didn't fully recover until many years after the bridge's construction.

After 14 years of construction, the Brooklyn Bridge opened on May 24, 1883. President Chester A. Arthur ambled across the bridge to meet Emily Roebling on the Brooklyn side. Today, the elegantly designed structure stands as one of the world's most recognizable landmarks.

Applicants for the job of painting the Brooklyn Bridge walk gingerly across the structure's suspension wires in 1926. Construction costs amounted to $15,211,982.92—an astronomical sum by 19th-century standards.

When the Brooklyn Bridge was built, its soaring towers were the city's tallest structures and its 3,460-foot span made it the longest suspension bridge in the world.

A poster advertises the opening of the Brooklyn Bridge on May 24, 1883. That day, more than 150,000 people and 1,800 vehicles crossed the engineering marvel. Fireworks lit up the sky that evening.

Left: In the foreground at left, a ferry is docked on the Brooklyn waterfront in 1888. One of the piers in the distance bears a sign reading, "Long Island Railroad Freight Depot." *Opposite:* Horse-drawn streetcars wait for passengers at the Fulton Ferry landing in the 1880s.

DUMBO

The Brooklyn neighborhood on the East River waterfront bounded by Fulton Street and the Brooklyn Navy Yard has undergone many transformations, and each time it has had an accompanying name change. For a time it was called Rapailie, the name of the landowners. Through the centuries, its name changed to Olympia, and later to Fulton Landing for the ferry that traversed the East River before the Brooklyn Bridge was built. Today, it is known as DUMBO. Although it sounds like a character in a children's movie, the name is an acronym of "Down Under the Manhattan Bridge Overpass."

At first a residential area, the character of the neighborhood began to change in the 1830s, when warehouses and factories were built. For much of the 19th and 20th centuries, the area was a large industrial center, consisting of factories and barren, cobblestone streets and piers on the waterfront. But in the late 1970s, artists and others looking for spacious residences moved into the expansive former industrial buildings-cum-loft spaces. In 2007, the New York City Landmarks Preservation Commission designated the area as a historic district. Various art galleries sprang up in the neighborhood, including the DUMBO Arts Center.

Today, the neighborhood draws both artists and families. In 2000, pastry chef Jacques Torres opened a waterfront chocolate factory, Jacques Torres D.U.M.B.O., in a converted brick warehouse on Water Street. On the same street, the Brooklyn Ice Cream Factory sells its freshly made sweet treats in a building that was once the Fulton Ferry Fire Boat House. The River Café, nestled under the Brooklyn Bridge, offers American cuisine served up with a view of the Manhattan skyline, and Grimaldi's Pizzeria offers some of the best Italian pies in New York City.

Treats 'n' Eats

With an unobstructed view of the Manhattan skyline across the East River, the Brooklyn Ice Cream Factory offers homemade icy treats. Diehard fans don't mind waiting in long lines for their favorite desserts at this former fire station near the Brooklyn Bridge.

At Jacques Torres D.U.M.B.O., chocolate lovers can swoon at the variety of the shop's handmade sweets and peek into the factory's windows to see how the sugary treats are made. At left, local DUMBO residents gather in the street during the summer to enjoy food and drink or just chat.

THE NYC SUBWAY SYSTEM

In the early 20th century, New York City's population of almost 3.5 million was one of the largest in the world. Many New Yorkers lived in crowded quarters, such as the Lower East Side, because it was difficult to work in Lower Manhattan and live elsewhere without efficient transportation. In March 1900, the privately owned Interborough Rapid Transit Company (IRT) solved this problem by building an underground train system.

The company hired 7,700 laborers to dig trenches and tunnels and place rails in underground train stations. The IRT line opened on October 27, 1904; that evening, 150,000 eager passengers each paid the five-cent fare. Before, traveling from Lower Manhattan to Harlem took several hours, but the IRT proudly boasted, "City Hall to Harlem in 15 minutes!" At the time, it was the world's fastest city transportation system.

Following the IRT's lead, the Brooklyn Rapid Transit Company (later the BMT) linked Manhattan and Brooklyn in 1915, and in 1932, NYC's Board of Transportation built its Independent City Owned Rapid Transit Railroad (IND). The city took over the IRT and BMT in 1940. But by 1968, the Metropolitan Transportation Authority (MTA) had taken over, and it continues to oversee the city's subways and buses to this day.

The NYC subway system currently consists of 468 stations, which is the largest number of public transit subway stations in the world. From the A train into Harlem to the Z train on Nassau Street, in 2007 the system transported more than 1.5 billion passengers.

In Brooklyn Heights, the New York Transit Museum operates in a former working subway station built in 1936. It chronicles the more than 100 years of NYC transit history through carefully preserved memorabilia, including more than 20 vintage subway cars and detailed mosaic tiles that once adorned the walls of early subway stations.

Above: The "el" trains—short for elevated trains—drove across tracks high above the bustling streets of the Bowery in the late 1890s. *Right:* From 1916 to 1932, New York City's subways were promoted as "The World's Safest Railroad." *The Subway Sun* encouraged passengers and subway employees to show "Courtesy from All to All."

Workmen make sure all bolts and caulking are secure as they labor on the Manhattan side of the East River tube in 1907.

NYC subways have a long tradition of elaborate tile mosaic artwork, some dating bac to the stations' earliest days. Even many directional signs, such as this one found in a Midtown station, were done in colorful ceramic patterns.

Passengers leave the Shuttle, a subway line that only travels from the Grand Central s to the Times Square stop and back again.

Right: A section of a subway map shows stations, including Grand Central and Times Square. When the first subways opened in 1904, the fare was five cents. Today's subway costs considerably more, and there are over 800 miles of subway lines that connect the various stops. *Below:* A guide at the Transit Museum gives visitors a tour of an actual vintage subway car.

Subway tokens in varying forms were used in New York City from the early 1950s until 2003, when they were discontinued and replaced by the MetroCard.

WILLIAMSBURG

In the 17th and 18th centuries, the area now known as Williamsburg was simple farmland on the East River. At the turn of the 19th century, a ferry operator named Richard M. Woodhull bought land there hoping to develop it into a town for commuters to Manhattan. He named the area Williamsburgh. When Woodhull's plans didn't materialize, however, he declared bankruptcy.

But his notions lived on. When a new turnpike was built connecting the coastal village to parts further inland, commuters considered living in the neighborhood. By the 1830s, businesses and residences were built by the likes of Commodore Vanderbilt and railroad magnate James Fisk.

In 1855, the village was incorporated into Brooklyn, and around the same time, the "h" in its name was dropped. A large influx of German immigrants arrived, many of whom opened breweries. In the early 1900s, Williamsburg's population included a great number of immigrants arriving from Eastern Europe and Italy. Many of the Italians came from the city of Nola, and they brought with them the annual religious Festa del Giglio. To this day, the festival fills the streets near Our Lady of Mount Carmel Church, where a towering 100-foot-tall statue is carried in a procession. Hasidic Jews also took up residence here in the 1930s, and the community still thrives in Williamsburg's south side.

Today, Italians and Hasidim share the neighborhood with Hispanic, Polish, and African Americans. As gentrification increased, young hipsters settled around Bedford Avenue. The old breweries are gone, but since 1996, the Brooklyn Brewery has called Williamsburg home. Deteriorating factories have been transformed into luxury condos, and Williamsburg's development continues.

Above: Opened on December 13, 1903, the Williamsburg Bridge spans the East River, connecting Manhattan and Brooklyn.
Right: Trolley lines fill the air at Metropolitan and Graham avenues in 1937 Williamsburg.

The Brooklyn Brewery, seen here in 2007, produces a number of core brands as well as seasonal beers. In the mid-1800s, German immigrants opened many breweries, including Samuel Liebmann (later called Rheingold Breweries) and the Schaefer Brewing Company, which moved its operations here from Manhattan.

A woman stands outside the entrance to the Bedford Avenue subway station in Williamsburg in 2008. The neighborhood's colorful setting has produced many famous natives, including Mel Brooks and Barbra Streisand.

BROOKLYN HEIGHTS

The area that comprises today's Brooklyn Heights was first inhabited by the native Canarsee peoples on the bluffs overlooking the East River. By the 1600s, it had become farmland for European settlers, and residents traveled to Manhattan via ferry.

When Robert Fulton's steam ferry began traversing the East River in 1814, the area attracted more settlers; it became an incorporated village soon after. In the 1820s, landowners, including Hezekiah Pierrepont, Henry Remsen, and John Hicks, moved to the area, and their memories live on in the form of street names. Throughout the 1800s, the number of residences grew, including the stately brownstones characteristic of this neighborhood. Soon, Brooklyn Heights had become a stylish quarter for residents with sophisticated tastes.

After the Interborough Rapid Transit opened a subway station in the Heights in 1908, it attracted a large population of commuters to Manhattan. Artists and those with literary aspirations began to call the Heights home. The moneyed residents resented the influx of have-nots, and many left the neighborhood. Some of their elegant mansions were turned into apartment buildings and boarding houses.

The neighborhood hit a slump during the Depression. In 1953, the construction of the Brooklyn-Queens Expressway called for the demolition of a large section of the Heights. But thanks to the efforts of groups such as the Brooklyn Heights Association and then-Parks Commissioner Robert Moses, the area was eventually restored to its former self. In 1950, the Brooklyn Heights Promenade (once known as the Esplanade) was built along the East River, high above the Brooklyn-Queens Expressway.

Today, the neighborhood has the charm of a small village, while being within short commuting distance of Manhattan. Young and old, middle class and affluent all call the Heights their home.

Top: This view from Brooklyn Heights in 1911 shows a burgeoning Manhattan across the river. *Above:* The Hotel St. George in Brooklyn Heights (here, as it looked in the early 1900s) was once the largest hotel in New York City. More than 2,000 rooms were spread out over a building complex that filled an entire city block. Today it is a residential co-op building.

Left: Horse-drawn buggies share the road with automobiles on Brooklyn's Willow and Poplar streets in 1936.

Above: The red-and-white Danish flag waves outside of the Danish Seamen's Church New York on Willow Street in Brooklyn Heights. Established in 1878 by Danish minister Rasmus Andersen, the church moved to its present location in 1957. The Lutheran house of worship is the only church in North and South America to hold services in Danish each Sunday. *Left:* A view from the Brooklyn Heights promenade. Photographed after the terrorist attacks, the Manhattan skyline in the distance is missing the World Trade Center's soaring Twin Towers.

BROOKLYN ACADEMY OF MUSIC (BAM)

Founded in 1861, the Brooklyn Academy of Music (BAM) is the oldest continuously operating performing arts center in the United States. Originally housed in a theater in Brooklyn Heights, the space was built as the home of the Philharmonic Society of Brooklyn.

A 1903 fire destroyed the theater, reducing the building to ashes. Three years later, a groundbreaking ceremony was held for a new theater at 30 Lafayette Avenue in Brooklyn's Fort Greene neighborhood, and the cornerstone was laid in place. In 1908, the building was completed, and a grand gala featured operatic luminaries Enrico Caruso and Geraldine Farrar in a performance of Gounod's *Faust*. The Metropolitan Opera continued to stage performances at the Brooklyn Academy of Music for the next 13 years.

Today's BAM consists of several venues near downtown Brooklyn. It has evolved into a vibrant urban arts center with national and international performing arts and film presentations. The facilities have been expanded to include the Howard Gilman Opera House, presenting concerts from classical to contemporary. Film festivals are held at BAM Rose Cinemas, and one of its screens is devoted to daily screenings of independent films.

The Lepercq Space was originally conceived as a ballroom, but the space is now home to the BAMcafé restaurant and a live music venue. An eclectic mix of dancers, musicians, and composers ranging from Philip Glass and Ingmar Bergman to Whirling Dervishes have presented here. Each Memorial Day weekend, BAM presents DanceAfrica, with dancers from around the world paying homage to African dance and music.

Above: In 1908, the Austin Organ Company installed this enormous organ at the concert hall at the Brooklyn Academy of Music. *Left:* In 1903, a fire destroyed the original Brooklyn Academy of Music on Montague Street (seen here in 1900).

Right: The Howard Gilman Opera House at the Brooklyn Academy of Music was designed by architects Henry Beaumont Herts and Hugh Tallant, who also created the Lyceum Theatre and the New Amsterdam Theatre. *Below:* The Restoration DanceAfrica Children's Ensemble performs at the Brooklyn Academy of Music.

This round window, called an "oculus," soars overhead at the Brooklyn Academy of Music.

THE BROOKLYN MUSEUM

One of the largest art museums in the United States, the Brooklyn Museum opened in 1897. Even so, the vast, 560,000-square-foot structure designed by McKim, Mead and White was originally meant to be six times its current size.

The museum houses more than one million objects from ancient masterpieces to more modern holdings. When the museum sponsored an expedition in southern Egypt from 1906 to 1908, it acquired various objects, including a terra-cotta figurine known as the "Bird Lady" from the pre-dynastic period over 5,000 years ago.

In 1923, the museum displayed one of the first exhibitions of African art in the United States, and it is still one of the largest exhibitions of its kind. The collection ranges from carved African masks to a meticulously beaded 19th-century Yoruba crown from Nigeria. American art holdings feature Edward Hicks's *The Peaceable Kingdom,* as well as 19th-century landscape and figure painters such as Frederic Church, Winslow Homer, and John Singer Sargent.

In the outdoor Steinberg Family Sculpture Garden, visitors view a display of sculptures, many of which were salvaged from iconic buildings on their way to being demolished. For example, Adolph A. Weinman's caped female sculpture, *Night,* was rescued from the old Pennsylvania Station, and four sculpted figures of Atlas are all that remain from a former 5th Avenue mansion. Contemporary art at the Brooklyn Museum ranges from a pink marble sculpture by Louise Bourgeois to the Willem de Kooning painting *Woman.* Max Weber and Georgia O'Keeffe are represented in the museum's collection of early modernist art.

In 2004, the museum received a new entrance pavilion of dazzling multistory sheer glass, bringing light into the grand 19th-century façade.

Above: The Brooklyn Museum, shown circa 1904, houses one of the largest and most diverse collections in the country.
Left: Daniel Chester French created sculptures of women (pictured in 1964) representing Brooklyn (left) and Manhattan for the front entrance of the Brooklyn Museum.

Among its varied collections, the Brooklyn Museum contains a world-renowned collection of ancient Egyptian art, including this room of artifacts and mummies, some dating to 1070 B.C. and older.

A 2008 exhibit featured Takashi Murakami's playful, 30-foot-tall *Reversed Double Helix*. Below, a detail of one of the five individual fiberglass sculptures that make up the piece.

CARNIVAL IN BROOKLYN

EVERY LABOR DAY WEEKEND, the musical sounds of calypso, soca, and more fill the air on Eastern Parkway. With its sizable Caribbean population, Brooklyn has hosted its annual West Indian Carnival Festival and Parade for over 40 years. Millions of onlookers attend the festival every year.

Gathered at the grounds of the Brooklyn Museum, the celebration is spread out over several days, and it features a number of events such as concerts with noted Caribbean musicians and singers and a steel band competition. The grand finale is the Labor Day Parade, with its procession of elaborate, multihued floats and dancers decked out in vibrantly colored costumes. The revelers strut down Eastern Parkway alongside musicians beating out hypnotic rhythms.

PROSPECT PARK

Built in mid-1860s, Prospect Park (once known as "Brooklyn's Jewel") was designed by architects Frederick Law Olmsted and Calvert Vaux. They had conceived the layout of Central Park in 1859 and learned much from that experience. Prospect Park's main features include the Long Meadow, an expansive 60-acre lake, and a tree-filled space called the Ravine. Today, Prospect Park is considered their masterpiece.

The duo envisioned it as a retreat for people from all walks of life, and they called for shaded arbors, graceful bridges, and majestic arches. There were originally even milk cows at a working dairy within the park.

In 1888, the city of Brooklyn, as it was then called, commissioned the architectural firm of McKim, Mead and White to redesign the park's entrances in the style of Europe's grand piazzas. Famed for their elaborate designs, including the original Pennsylvania Station and the Washington Square Arch, the firm added soaring pillars and grandiose pavilions. In addition, in 1869, John H. Duncan, who created Grant's Tomb in Manhattan, was asked to design a huge arch gracing the park's entryway—the Grand Army Plaza.

During the 1960s, the park fell into decline and was in dire need of repair. With the help of then-Mayor Ed Koch and former Parks Commissioner Gordon Davis, the city allotted $10 million for the park's restoration.

Today, the park welcomes visitors to 585 acres of rolling meadows, Brooklyn's only forest, and a Beaux Arts–style boathouse. From outdoor art exhibitions and free concerts, including those by Metropolitan Opera stars, to the indoor Tennis Center and the wintertime skating rink, Prospect Park offers a wealth of activities for visitors.

Above: The plan for Prospect Park, as seen in 1901. *Left:* Young visitors to Prospect Park in the 1930s sit near the bronze plaque of Lafayette and Washington at the 9th Street entrance.

Visitors park their vehicle in Grand Army Plaza, the front entrance to Prospect Park, in 1903. Architect John H. Duncan designed the Soldiers' and Sailors' Memorial Arch, which was completed in 1892.

Left: Edwin Clarke Litchfield, a lawyer and owner of a plot of land that would become part of Prospect Park, had this villa built in 1857. Today it is the Brooklyn headquarters of the NYC Department of Parks & Recreation.

Right: The nation's first urban Audubon Center, based in Prospect Park, is dedicated to educating the public about the natural world and to preserving wildlife. The waterside building is a historic New York City Landmark. Visitors can glide along on the center's electric boat tours on the *Independence,* passing under historic bridges and lush landscapes.

Colorful autumn leaves and a stone path create a stunning backdrop for the pond at Prospect Park's boathouse.

MAUSOLEUMS AND MONUMENTS

NOT FAR FROM PROSPECT PARK lies a national landmark, the Green-Wood Cemetery. Opened in 1838, the cemetery is the final resting place of close to 600,000 people in over 478 acres of greenery. Four limpid lakes punctuate thousands of trees, tranquil pathways, and rolling hillsides. Red-tailed hawks, willow flycatchers, gulls, and other birds soar above the grounds of this peaceful area.

The cemetery is currently open to visitors every day of the week. During the 19th century, Green-Wood was one of the most popular tourist attractions in the United States, with hundreds of thousands of visitors strolling through the grounds. Among the famous people buried here are Elias Howe, the inventor of the sewing machine (as well as his dog, Fannie); noted conductor and composer Leonard Bernstein; artist Lewis Comfort Tiffany; and abolitionist Henry Ward Beecher.

BROOKLYN BOTANIC GARDEN

Since 1910, the Brooklyn Botanic Garden has attracted visitors from near and far who seek its lush, living landscape of plant collections and specialty gardens. With over 10,000 species of flora, the garden's 52 acres brim with blooms, both native and from around the world. Among the highlights is the C. V. Starr Bonsai Museum, which houses the second largest publicly displayed collection of miniature trees outside of Japan.

The Fragrance Garden, opened in 1955, was the first garden in the United States specifically designed for the sight-impaired (though created to be enjoyed by all visitors). There, labels appear in Braille, and plants like Indian patchouli and lemon verbena are selected for their perfumed scents. Richly textured leaves like those found on lamb's ears and curly mint plants were included to give visitors a tactile experience.

Each spring, the Japanese Hill-and-Pond Garden is host to Sakura Matsuri, the Japanese cherry blossom festival. There, visitors take in the wondrous display as the branches of over 200 of these graceful trees fill with pale green buds that transform into bright pink blossoms. One can also find the Shakespeare Garden, an Elizabethan exhibit that features more than 80 plant species mentioned in the Bard's writings, including Cupid's Dart and Queen-of-the-Prairie.

The Garden's Steinhardt Conservatory is home to a vast indoor plant collection featuring tropical, warm temperate, and desert plants. The Robert W. Wilson Aquatic House brims with delicate orchids, delicate tropical water plants, and even fragrant but dangerous carnivorous plants.

The Brooklyn Botanic Garden (seen here in 1922) was founded on the site of a former ash dump. Now water lilies bloom in serene ponds, and visitors can enjoy the lush greenery.

Japanese Hill-and-Pond Garden

In this photo from 1925, a Japanese woman in her native attire strolls by a teahouse as visitors watch. Japanese landscape designer Takeo Shiota came to America in 1907 to create, "a garden more beautiful than all others in the world."

In early summer, visitors can find the Cranford Rose Garden in full bloom at the Brooklyn Botanic Garden.

CONEY ISLAND

From the 1890s until World War I, Coney Island was synonymous with the phrase "amusement parks." In 1895, Steeplechase Park offered plenty of high-adrenaline fun, including rides on speeding mechanical horses along undulating tracks. Across from Steeplechase, Luna Park featured rides such as the Dragon's Gorge, which thrilled visitors with simulated scenes both real and mythical, such as the Grand Canyon and the River Styx. Dreamland opened in 1904 with attractions that included gondolas on a simulated Grand Canal and trains crossing a model of the Alps, complete with blasts of icy air. Dreamland's 375-foot tower boasted twin searchlights that could be spotted far out at sea.

Unfortunately, the excessive delights of Coney Island's amusement parks didn't last forever. Raging fires closed down Dreamland in 1911 and Luna Park in 1944. The New York Aquarium now stands on Dreamland's former site. Steeplechase prospered for 67 years, but it closed its doors in 1964.

Today, crowds still stroll down the boardwalk, originally built in 1923. KeySpan Park opened in 2001 on Steeplechase Park's former site. The Brooklyn Cyclones, a minor-league baseball team, still call the 7,500-seat stadium home. The original Nathan's hot dog stand, founded in 1916, still sells its famous frankfurters, which have been enjoyed by Cary Grant, Jacqueline Kennedy, and other luminaries.

Three historic rides remain and are now designated New York City landmarks. Thrill-seekers can still ride the Cyclone roller coaster or take a lazy trip on the 150-foot historic Ferris wheel, which holds 144 people at once, at Deno's Wonder Wheel Amusement Park. And although it is currently closed, the towering Parachute Jump still soars above the beach as a monument to Coney Island's storied past.

Luna Park

The fairy-tale towers and fantasy-filled structures of Luna Park (top) drew large crowds to its many attractions, including exotic minarets and a resident herd of elephants. Luna Park (as seen from the street) delighted visitors from 1903 until its closing in 1944. One of the owners named the sprawling amusement park after his sister, Luna.

Above: During the Fourth of July weekend, 1938, those who couldn't afford to leave the sweltering temperatures of the city flocked to the beach at Coney Island to cool off. Police estimated that one million sun seekers packed the beach that weekend.
Right: This smiling fella has been the mascot for George C. Tilyou's Steeplechase Park at Coney Island since the 1890s.

Visitors sunbathe and swim at Coney Island. At right is the famous Cyclone roller coaster, the source of many yelps and screams since 1927.

The colorful Coney Island Mermaid Parade has been celebrated every summer since 1983. Lovely ladies of the sea strut (or are carried on floats) down the boardwalk as an appreciative crowd looks on.

THE NEW YORK AQUARIUM

From sea lions to beluga whales and from electric eels to hefty walruses, more than 350 species and 8,000 specimens of sea creatures splash, waddle, and swim in the New York Aquarium located in Coney Island. The facility is the oldest continually operating aquarium in the United States. On December 10, 1896, the aquarium opened its doors to the public at its original location in Castle Clinton at the southern tip of Manhattan. With just 150 specimens at the time, the first aquarium's inhabitants were eventually relocated in 1941 as a result of the construction on the Brooklyn-Battery Tunnel. The animals were temporarily housed in the Bronx Zoo until the new facility was ready.

Run by the Wildlife Conservations Society, the present-day New York Aquarium opened in 1957 on the Coney Island boardwalk as part of a revitalization effort for the area. The $9 million facility required over one million gallons of water to keep the thousands of specimens in their re-created environments.

The aquarium continues to follow its mission of raising the public's awareness about issues concerning the ocean and its many inhabitants through research, public events, and special exhibits. Every day, visitors can watch the aquarium's trainers feeding sea otters, penguins, sharks, walruses, and other animal residents.

Conservation Hall features a 165,000-gallon tank brimming with more than 35 species, including sharks and moray eels. The nearby Sea Cliffs exhibit recreates a 300-foot-long rocky coastline for resident penguins and marine mammals. The Aquatheater features various daily shows, including marine mammal training sessions. Meanwhile, the *Seahorses!* exhibit includes some surprise specimens of the tiny horse-headed creatures, such as the leafy sea dragon and the weedy sea dragon, which blend into the background of leafy plants in their tank.

Top: An illustration from 1915 shows the former New York Aquarium building in 1850, then known as Castle Garden. *Bottom:* A sea-themed mural adds a splash of color to Coney Island Boardwalk.

BRIGHTON BEACH

Between Coney Island and Manhattan Beach, the Brighton Beach neighborhood lies next to the Atlantic Ocean, with broad stretches of soft sand and bustling streets farther inland. Its first developer, William A. Engeman, began transforming the area into a summer vacation community in 1868. Ten years later, investors paid for the construction of the stylish Hotel Brighton, calling the area Brighton Beach after a fashionable seaside resort town in England. One year later, a racetrack was built, and in 1907, the opening of the Brighton Beach Baths increased the area's popularity. Modest seaside cottages filled up during the summer months.

By the 1930s, dozens of apartment buildings had been built, and a largely European Jewish population moved in. Four decades later, however, the town was beginning to decline. Garbage was strewn in the streets and graffiti marred buildings. Many second-generation residents moved out, and their elderly parents were left behind, frightened by the rising crime rate. Inspired, a young mother named Pat Singer organized the Brighton Beach Association, and the group gradually took back the neighborhood.

In the 1980s, Brighton Beach experienced an influx of immigrants from the Soviet Union. Since then, the area's nickname has been "Little Odessa by the Sea," after the many residents originally from the Ukrainian city on the Black Sea.

Today's Brighton Beach boasts upscale condominiums that have replaced the old summer cottages. The main thoroughfare, Brighton Beach Avenue, is lined with stores with signs in Cyrillic located under the rumbling elevated subway tracks. Nightclubs feature Russian entertainers, and food stores sell savory blini (Russian pancakes) with sour cream and caviar, as well as other favorites. In addition to the Russian population, present-day Brighton Beach is home to other ethnic populations, including Pakistani, Polish, Turkish, Mexican, Chinese, and Korean residents.

In the late 1880s, Brighton Beach had two vaudeville theaters, and even was the scene of a Buffalo Bill spectacular. Here, bathers relax at Brighton Beach in the early 1900s.

Moving Day

In 1888, the three-story, 174-room Brighton Beach Hotel was jacked up, placed on railroad cars, and moved 600 feet inland. The next year, it served as the backdrop for a September 1889 luncheon honoring women's rights activist Susan B. Anthony.

With plenty to do and see, and the Brighton Beach subway station nearby, the neighborhood remains a popular weekend getaway for many New Yorkers.

Above: "Little Odessa by the Sea," a.k.a. Brighton Beach, is home to many Russian-speaking immigrants. It's easy to find dumplings, borscht, and other delicacies in the neighborhood's cafés.

The Bronx

ON THE MAINLAND

Nothing says "out-of-towner" to a New Yorker's ears faster than someone talking about "Bronx" instead of using the correct term, "*the* Bronx," to refer to the city's northernmost borough. In fact, the Bronx is the only New York borough that is on the mainland of the United States.

The Bronx has certainly seen some changes over the years, transforming from an area of densely forested hills and valleys to a densely populated borough with urban oases such as Van Cortlandt Park, Henry Hudson Park, and Pelham Bay Park.

The Bronx of today has plenty to offer. The New York Botanical Garden is home to the world's largest Victorian glasshouse, and the world-famous Bronx Zoo is the largest urban zoo in the United States. The borough also boasts its own Little Italy on Arthur Avenue, where pastry shops such as Artuso's have delighted customers with their rich Italian desserts: cannolis, tiramisu, and sfogliatelle. The Riverdale section of the Bronx is known for its upscale housing and outstanding Hudson River views.

BECOMING A BOROUGH

Like the other four NYC boroughs, the first inhabitants of the Bronx were the Paleo-Indians. Later, the Algonquin-speaking inhabitants, the Lenape, made the area their home thousands of years before any Europeans set foot in the region. In an attempt to find a northern route between Europe and Asia, in 1609 English explorer Henry Hudson and his crew sailed Hudson's ship, the *Half Moon*, into the river that now bears his name. It is said that he may have at one point anchored at Spuyten Duyvil Creek to weather a storm; today that area is in the Riverdale section of the Bronx.

The Bronx was named after a Danish sea captain, Jonas Bronck, who was the first European settler in the area. In 1639, Bronck, his wife, and their indentured servants

After the Civil War, City Island in the Bronx became a shipbuilding hub, in particular leisure and racing yachts. These shipyard workers are seen working on a vessel in the early 20th century.

Opposite: Visitors view elephants and other animals at the Bronx Zoo in 1911.

settled on a farm on land between what is now the Harlem River and another river the Lenape referred to as *Aquehung* (now known as the Bronx River).

By the 1800s, the area was an agrarian community with some small villages and a number of country estates. The Bronx did not become a borough of New York City at once. Western parts of the area joined the city in 1874, followed by the eastern areas in 1895. In 1898, when the rest of the boroughs were consolidated into Greater New York City, the already-annexed areas of the Bronx became a New York City borough.

During the 19th century, the Bronx's population began to increase following the arrival of German immigrants, as well as the Irish immigrants who were escaping the potato famine in their own country. As these Europeans flocked to the New World, thousands of them decided to settle in the Bronx.

INTO THE 20TH CENTURY

The late 1900s brought an influx of Italian immigrants to the Bronx, and they left their mark on what is now a smaller-size Little Italy on Arthur Avenue in the Belmont section of the borough. In 1904, extensions of the existing subways in Manhattan linked it to the Bronx; these connections resulted in a new population of commuters who lived in the Bronx and worked in Manhattan.

Jews were among the ethnic groups that settled in the borough at this time. Many of them had previously lived with their families in small, dim, overcrowded Manhattan tenements, and in the Bronx's expansion, they saw an opportunity to live in the larger, newly built apartments.

After World War II, the Bronx experienced an expansion of its housing, and the ethnic groups that were strongly represented in the early days began to dwindle in numbers. Presently, the borough is home to a large population of Dominicans and Puerto Ricans, as well as African Americans. Other ethnic groups in the borough today include Greeks, Russians, Vietnamese, Pakistanis, and Koreans. The Bronx also boasts its share of cultural contributions: It is recognized as the birthplace of hip-hop music and was the home of pop star Jennifer Lopez, designer Ralph Lauren, and film director Stanley Kubrick.

Like Brooklyn, the Bronx has played a great role in the all-American sport of baseball. The original Yankee Stadium opened on April 18, 1923, as the home of the New York Yankees. Tens of thousands of fans packed the arena, and thousands more stood outside its gates. On that day, baseball legend Babe Ruth hit the stadium's first home run and followed it with two more home runs to lead the Yankees to a 4–1 victory against the Boston Red Sox. The beloved ballpark continued to host memorable games for 85 years. It was demolished and later replaced by the new Yankee Stadium, which opened in 2009.

HIP-HOP: BORN IN THE BRONX

THE DYNAMIC MUSIC KNOWN AS HIP-HOP may be famous throughout the world, but many musicologists pinpoint its roots back to the Bronx. In the early 1970s, an energetic Caribbean-born DJ spun records in an apartment building for lower- and middle-class residents, located at the now-legendary address of 1520 Sedgwick Avenue. Clive Campbell, better known under his hip-hop moniker, DJ Kool Herc (shown here in more recent times) had come up with an innovative style of presenting music by manipulating his turntables to extend and repeat existing breaks in funk songs. Crowds of dancers loved Herc's groundbreaking flow, and other DJs built on his musical foundation. Hip-hop's popularity spread, and a genre was born.

Despite protests from residents, the Sedgwick Avenue apartment complex was sold in October 2008. Residents had hoped to preserve the historical nature of the building.

Lush palm trees and brightly colored flowers thrive at the New York Botanical Garden.

YANKEE STADIUM

On April 18, 1923, the iconic Yankee Stadium opened in the South Bronx to a roaring crowd of over 74,000 ardent fans. The home of the New York Yankees, the famed ballpark was constructed on land purchased from the estate of financier William Waldorf Astor.

The stadium was affectionately referred to as "The House That Ruth Built" in honor of Babe Ruth, the baseball star who wowed crowds of onlookers with his home runs in this world-famous ballpark. Known as "The Sultan of Swat," Ruth was left-handed, and most of his home run hits went sailing over the right field grandstands. These areas became known as "Ruthville." Over the years, many of baseball's legends, including Joe DiMaggio, Mickey Mantle, Lou Gehrig, and Roger Maris, played at Yankee Stadium.

Baseball fans continued to flock to Yankee Stadium until September 21, 2008, when the last game was played there. A crowd of 54,000 nostalgic fans looked on as Babe Ruth's 92-year-old daughter, Julia Ruth Stevens, stood up from her wheelchair and tossed the ceremonial first pitch for the final game. The Yankees left the stadium in the same way they came in: as winners, beating the Baltimore Orioles 7–3.

Construction began on a new stadium in 2006, across the street from the site of the former ballpark. Groundbreaking ceremonies for the new ballpark were held on August 16, 2006, to coincide with the anniversary of Ruth's death. The newly constructed venue opened in 2009, taking the name of the original stadium. And talk about inflation: The original Yankee Stadium cost $2.5 million to build in the 1920s, but the current park's price tag was more than $1.5 billion.

Right: In 1921, the year this photo was taken, Yankees star Babe Ruth set a new single-season home run record—for the third season in a row.

The Ol' Ballpark

Left: The New York Yankees' first stadium was at the American League Park (nicknamed Hilltop Park) in Washington Heights, Manhattan. At the time, the Yankees were known as the New York Highlanders. The Yankees had their last game at the ballpark in 1912, then played at the Polo Grounds for many years. In 1923, the original Yankee Stadium opened in the Bronx, and the team finally had a home to call their own.

Right: The new Yankee Stadium, as seen in 2009, will be able to hold more than 52,000 spectators. *Below:* Within the stadium, the concourse features soaring, light-filled ceilings, banners picturing Yankee greats, and more amenities.

CITY ISLAND

Connected to the mainland area of the Bronx by a small bridge, City Island has long been a nautical community. Surrounded by Eastchester Bay on the east and flanked by Long Island Sound on the west, the mile-long island was first inhabited by the Siwanoy, a people who called the land Minnewit. They spent their summers here, feasting on the abundance of oysters, clams, and other seafood thriving in the island's waters.

In 1614, explorer Adriaen Block claimed the island for the Dutch, and European colonists settled in the area. In 1654, Thomas Pell, an Englishman, bought land from the Siwanoy. The Dutch governor, Peter Stuyvesant, unsuccessfully attempted to force Pell and his family to leave, but they continued to own the island for many years.

By the 1700s, the island was home to many oystermen and pilots who helped to navigate ships that were passing through the East River and its treacherous Hell Gate section to New York Harbor. At this time, it was known as Minneford Island.

In 1761, Benjamin Palmer bought the land and renamed it New City Island. Hoping to establish the tiny harbor as a major city, he launched two ferries and set up a grid of streets. Although never a rival to Manhattan as Palmer had hoped, City Island became an important center of shipbuilding and yachting. The island also played a valuable role in New York's defense because of its strategic position. In 1896, City Island became part of New York City.

Today, the picturesque island resembles a quiet New England fishing village. Its main street, City Island Avenue, is filled with seafood restaurants, marinas, yacht clubs, and marine supply stores. Locals and visitors alike enjoy the views from City Island Park, facing Eastchester Bay. Bird-watching is also a popular activity. On weekends, mainlanders drive to the island and frequent the many waterfront bars, restaurants, and cafés.

A vintage look at City Island Avenue, the island's main street, which still features stores and restaurants to this day.

The Shipyard

Workers tow a mast at the former Henry B. Nevins Yacht Builders yard. Nevins opened his business in 1907 on City Island. The business closed in 1962; the site is now the home of the City Island Elementary School.

City Island's long history of sailing continues to this day as weekenders find a relaxing escape sailboating.

THE BRONX ZOO

South of the New York Botanical Garden, the sprawling, 265-acre Bronx Zoo is the largest metropolitan zoo in the United States. Nearby Fordham University once owned most of the land that became the zoo and the New York Botanical Garden, but it was sold to the City of New York for $1 with the stipulation that the land would only be used for these two city projects.

In 1896, zoologist William Hornaday became the director of the zoo project, and architects George Heins and Christopher LaFarge laid out designs for the first permanent buildings. In 1899, the New York Zoological Park, later known as the Bronx Zoo, opened its doors. In its earliest days, it featured a primate house, an elephant house, a lion house, and many Beaux Arts–style buildings.

Hornaday was an expert on American bison, which by that time had been hunted nearly to extinction. At his insistence, the zoo included a bison breeding ground. In 1907, 15 bison bred at the Bronx Zoo were sent to Oklahoma's Wichita Mountain Preserve to help increase their numbers. Today, about 20,000 bison roam in the American West. In fact, bison herds at Yellowstone National Park and elsewhere can trace their lineage to the herd raised in the Bronx Zoo.

The zoo is now home to thousands of animals, with special areas such as the Congo Gorilla Forest, where groups of animals roam free in a re-created rainforest much like their native jungles. In the *African Plains* exhibit, lions roar and giraffes gracefully amble up to trees for a leafy lunch. Opened in 2008, the zoo's *Madagascar!* exhibit features leaping lemurs, slithering tree boas, and hissing cockroaches, all against a background of towering baobab trees and forested deserts from the island of Madagascar.

The sculpted heads of an elephant and a rhinoceros grace an archway on a building in the Bronx Zoo.

Above: Visitors take a little stroll at the zoo in 1943. *Left:* In 1947, a zookeeper at the Bronx Zoo hands a "birthday cake" of alfalfa and carrot "candles" to Pete the hippopotamus to celebrate the hippo's birthday.

An aerial view of the Bronx Zoo, part of the Wildlife Conservation Society, shows the huge green expanses that are home to many animals, including some endangered species such as the hairy rhino and the snow leopard.

More than 20 western lowland gorillas roam free in the Bronx Zoo's Congo Gorilla Forest. Sturdy glass panels allow visitors to view the gorillas in their re-created habitat.

EDGAR ALLAN POE COTTAGE

Edgar Allan Poe, famed author of American Gothic poetry and tales, lived in a small farmhouse in the Bronx from 1846 to 1849. His young wife, Virginia, was gravely ill with tuberculosis, and Poe hoped that moving from their former home in urban Manhattan to the serene setting in the Bronx would help her recover. From their modest cottage in the rural village of Fordham, they could look out over verdant hills. Across the road, colorful apple blossoms bloomed in an orchard, and the country air and serene setting was in sharp contrast to Manhattan's busy streets.

Poe wrote some of his most famous poems while living in the little white cottage on Kingsbridge Road, including "Annabel Lee," "Eureka," and "The Bells." He filled his days with writing and gardening, and he often visited and conversed with the Jesuits at neighboring St. John's College, now Fordham University.

Despite the move, Virginia passed away in the cottage in 1847. Heartbroken, Poe died two years later in Baltimore, Maryland.

When Kingsbridge Road was widened in 1895, the house was in danger of demolition. However, the New York Shakespeare Society petitioned the New York State legislature to save the structure. The area's former apple orchard was transformed into Poe Park in 1902.

The cottage was eventually moved across the road to its current site, and on November 15, 1913, the cottage was opened to the public. The dedication ceremony included a reading of Poe's poem "The Raven." Poe Park soon held classical music concerts, with large audiences in attendance. From the 1940s through the '60s, concerts included many popular big band and jazz musicians of the time, such as Benny Goodman, Glen Miller, and Jimmy Dorsey.

The building is now on the National Register of Historic Places. Period furniture graces the interior, and guided tours describe the tragic life of this talented writer.

Above left: The Poe Cottage as it looked in 1900. The one-and-a-half-story building was typical of the workmen's residences that were at one time common in the Bronx. The small structure still stands today and is the sole remaining house from the old village of Fordham. *Above:* The Poe Cottage in the Bronx.

THE NEW YORK BOTANICAL GARDEN

In the late 19th century, botanists Elizabeth and Nathaniel Lord Britton returned from their visit to England's Royal Botanic Gardens with a plan: to campaign for a garden in NYC that would rival those they saw in England. Their efforts paid off; on April 28, 1891, the state legislature passed an act establishing the New York Botanical Garden. Land was granted from the former estate of tobacco magnate Pierre Lorillard, and some of the funding came from wealthy donors including J. P. Morgan, Andrew Carnegie, and Cornelius Vanderbilt.

Now a designated National Historic Landmark, the botanical garden in the northern Bronx functions as a museum of living plant collections open to the public, an educational institution for children and adults, and a plant research center. Open year-round, the garden encompasses a vast 250-acre landscape, 50 display gardens, and a 50-acre native forest, the last remnants of New York City's original trees. Over one million plants, from delicate orchids to towering evergreens, thrive here. A section of the Bronx River runs through the gardens, and waterfalls cascade in the serene landscape.

One of the highlights of the garden is the beautifully designed Enid A. Haupt Conservatory. Its spacious interior houses plants from around the world, with different sections highlighting flora from a variety of climates. One section boasts the lush, living landscape of a tropical rainforest, with a staircase winding upward among the exotic trees so visitors can have a bird's-eye view of the palm trees and bromeliads that grow here.

At left is the dome of the Enid A. Haupt Conservatory, seen here in 1938. The glasshouse features plants from different climate zones around the world and includes an indoor re-creation of an Amazon rainforest, replete with live orchids, tall trees, and hanging plants. The conservatory is the largest Victorian-era glasshouse in the United States.

The New York Botanical Garden's LuEsther T. Mertz Library houses one of the largest and most significant botanical research libraries in the world.

Water lilies bloom in the summer in ponds near the Enid A. Haupt Conservatory glasshouse.

A whimsical topiary creation blooms at the New York Botanical Garden in 2005.

Above: A miniature train rolls past a scale model of the original 1923 Yankee Stadium at the New York Botanical Garden's annual Holiday Train Show. *Left:* The Bronx River flows through the garden's tranquil landscapes.

WAVE HILL

In the affluent Riverdale section of the Bronx, Wave Hill lies perched upon a hillside overlooking the Hudson River. Facing the Palisades across the water, the 28-acre public garden and cultural center offers spectacular views of the steep cliffs on the New Jersey side of the river.

Built in 1843 as the country home of jurist William Lewis Morris, the property was later owned by publisher William Henry Appleton from 1866 until 1903. In 1903, the property changed hands once more, and George W. Perkins, a partner of J. P. Morgan, became the owner. Perkins purchased adjacent riverside properties and developed his estate in the Hudson Highlands into blossoming gardens and meandering paths to complement its stunning cliffside panoramas. As a private residence, Wave Hill House hosted famous guests including Charles Darwin, Mark Twain, and Arturo Toscanini.

In 1960, the Perkins family deeded the property to New York City, and Wave Hill entered its present phase as a public garden. The great lawn's pergola overlook is a favorite place for visitors to view the striking scenery across the water. Upper pergolas also wrap around two gardens, including one featuring aquatic plants and grasses. The Marco Polo Stufano Conservatory houses flora from around the world, and the Palm House features an indoor garden that safely thrives throughout the icy New York City winters.

Along the hillside, a wild garden sprawls with bright blossoms. A Georgian Revival–style building circa 1927 is home to the Glyndor Gallery, where contemporary art exhibits are held. Surrounding the stately gardens is the Herbert and Hyonja Abrons Woodland, with a trail leading into its ten acres of meadow and woodland, brimming with native trees and colorful wildflowers.

Above: The flower-filled gardens of Wave Hill offer a breathtaking view of the Hudson River and the 500-foot-tall Palisades Cliffs in the distance. *Right:* Wave Hill House was leased in 1870–1871 to New York banker Theodore Roosevelt Sr. and his family. His son Theodore Roosevelt Jr. later went on to become the 26th president of the United States.

Staten Island

AN ISLAND APART

Located in New York Harbor where Upper New York Bay meets Lower New York Bay, Staten Island is the only outer borough that is not directly linked to Manhattan by bridges, tunnels, or subways. Connected to Brooklyn by the massive Verrazano-Narrows Bridge, which opened in 1964, Staten Island's only other outside connections are three bridges that lead to nearby New Jersey. To make the journey to and from the island, an annual 20 million commuters and visitors take the five-mile, 25-minute Staten Island Ferry ride to the terminal on Whitehall Street at the southern tip of Manhattan.

With a smaller population and a more suburban atmosphere than NYC's other four boroughs, Staten Island is also distinguishable by its unique topography. The borough offers plenty of natural beauty: The 2,800-acre Greenbelt features a number of trails, and a wealth of other parkland covers hunderds of acres. Blue Heron Park sprawls across more than 200 acres, with wetland ponds, swamps, and streams that play home to blue herons and other birds.

While much of the island has flat expanses of pristine greenery and an extensive shoreline, Staten Island also boasts a ridge of steep hills not found elsewhere in the city. The island's upscale Todt Hill section, rising 409 feet above sea level, is actually the highest point on the East Coast south of Maine.

Opposite: The Staten Island Ferry *President Roosevelt* pulls into the Battery Maritime Building on Whitehall Street in 1924.

Although it is probably the least publicized of the boroughs, Staten Island offers plenty of unexpected attractions. The island has a thriving cultural scene, with multiple museums—including several at the Snug Harbor Cultural Center complex. Another popular site is Fort Wadsworth, built in the 17th century, which stands as one of the oldest military fortifications in the nation.

GOING DUTCH
Like the other boroughs, the area that later became Staten Island was initially inhabited by Native Americans. In the early 17th century, Dutch colonists made several failed attempts at settling on the island but were unsuccessful at taking over the land from the Lenape peoples who lived there. The Dutch and the Lenape engaged in three (colorfully

In this photo from the early 20th century, retired sailors amuse themselves with games of cribbage and dominoes at what was then known as Sailor's Snug Harbor.

named) wars over the area: the Pig War in 1641, the Whiskey War in 1642, and the Peach War in 1655.

The Dutch finally succeeded in establishing their first permanent settlement in 1661, and more settlements soon followed. The Dutch called the island "Staten Eylandt," with a nod to the *Staten-Generaal* or Estate General, the parliament of the Netherlands at the time. True to the diversity that has always been a part of New York City, the early colonists were not only Dutch, but also British, French Huguenots, and eventually, African slaves.

THE BRITS TAKE CHARGE

After the Dutch surrendered to the British in 1664, Staten Island became part of the province of New York. In 1683 it became known as the County of Richmond. The name honored the Duke of Richmond, an illegitimate son of the English King Charles II. (The

Duke of Richmond was also an ancestor of Princess Diana.) The island's growth increased under British rule, but it remained an agrarian community. The population mainly subsisted on farming, the milling of flour, and a burgeoning fishing industry, which took advantage of the bounty of the surrounding waters—particularly its wealth of shellfish.

During the Revolutionary War, the island was of strategic importance. General George Washington used Staten Island's harbor as a vantage point to await the arrival of the British. On September 11, 1776, British Admiral Lord Howe set up a meeting with Benjamin Franklin, John Adams, and Edward Rutledge in a desperate attempt to prevent war. Ultimately, negotiations failed, and war became inevitable. Colonel Christopher Billopp, a Loyalist on Staten Island, offered his manor house as the site for the covert meeting; today it is known as the Conference House,

an integral part of Staten Island's Conference House Park.

STATEN ISLAND, U.S.A.

In 1898, when the other boroughs became part of New York City, Staten Island followed suit. Some Staten Islanders were against the idea; they considered becoming an independent city, but they failed to win support for their idea.

In the 1980s, Staten Island's desire to secede arose once again. In 1993, 65 percent of Staten Island residents voted in a nonbinding referendum to secede from New York City. Although the State Senate subsequently passed a bill allowing the move, it was blocked in the State Assembly and the secession never came to pass.

BRIDGING THE GAP

One of the greatest influences on Staten Island's growth from a rural farming community to a bustling, modern area was the completion of the Verrazano-Narrows Bridge in 1964. The opening of this suspension bridge leading to Brooklyn led to a migration of thousands of Brooklynites to Staten Island, many of them Italians and Italian Americans.

This, combined with improvements in public transportation (in particular the Staten Island Ferry), helped spur the evolution of this quiet agricultural community to an island of suburban neighborhoods and some industry. Today's Staten Island still has a strong Italian American population, but other ethnic groups, particularly Russians, have also made the island their home.

The St. George Theatre gleams in all its glory after a complete restoration, which cost more than $1 million.

The Jacques Marchais Museum of Tibetan Art, located on Lighthouse Hill in Staten Island, features rare Buddhist art and buildings that resemble a Tibetan Himalayan monastery.

WHO INVENTED THE TELEPHONE?

EVERYONE KNOWS THAT ALEXANDER GRAHAM BELL was the inventor of the telephone—or was he? According to historians, Antonio Meucci, an Italian immigrant and Staten Island resident, may have devised the telephone years before Bell.

Born in Italy in 1808, Meucci worked as a stage technician at the Teatro della Pergola in Florence. He devised a rudimentary "pipe telephone" that allowed theater workers to communicate from distances. After living in Cuba, Meucci moved to Staten Island in 1850. When his wife became ill in 1855, he set up a system linking her sickbed with his workshop. Unable to afford the entire U.S. patent application process, Meucci filed a caveat—a one-year, renewable intention to patent. When that ran out, however, he could not afford to renew it.

Seeking financial backing, he sent a model of his "teletrofono" to Western Union but was later told that they lost it. Just two years later, Bell, who conducted experiments in the same laboratory as Meucci, filed a patent for the telephone.

Meucci sued, and in 1887, the U.S. government moved to annul Bell's patent on the grounds of "fraud and misrepresentation." Meucci died in 1889, and Bell's patent expired in 1893. The case was eventually dropped.

SNUG HARBOR CULTURAL CENTER

In 1801, Captain Robert Richard Randall created the first three buildings in what would later become the Snug Harbor Cultural Center—"a haven for aged, decrepit and worn out sailors." Over the course of a century, the retired sailors' home expanded to 50 structures populated by 900 residents from around the world. By the late 1800s, the community boasted its own blacksmith shop, bakery, dairy, and a working farm that sustained residents. Dining halls and dormitories were housed in five expansive buildings, and a music hall provided entertainment.

By the mid-1900s, however, Snug Harbor experienced financial difficulties, and buildings such as the once-gleaming white marble Randall Memorial Church began to deteriorate and were demolished. Coming to Snug Harbor's rescue, the New York City Landmarks Commission saved the remaining buildings, which are some of the best examples of Greek Revival structures in the United States. Now a Smithsonian Affiliate,

the Snug Harbor Cultural Center & Botanical Garden is an 83-acre complex housing several major organizations, as well as a music hall, the VMH playhouse, and a formal Tuscan garden designed to resemble an Italian villa. The Botanical Garden boasts the New York Chinese Scholar's Garden, which features eight meditative pavilions with two main courtyards designed by the Landscape Architecture Corporation of China. The serene space resembles a tranquil Chinese watercolor landscape.

Also located on the grounds of Snug Harbor, Staten Island Children's Museum delights young visitors with games and hands-on exhibits. Visitors can also enjoy the Noble Maritime Collection, which is dedicated to the art, writing, and maritime artifacts of maritime artist John A. Noble. The Newhouse Center for Contemporary Art displays changing exhibits of modern and contemporary artists. In 2009, the Staten Island Museum took up residence in Snug Harbor; there, visitors can learn about the history of the borough and its people.

Above left: The Music Hall, seen here in the early 20th century, is considered the second-oldest music hall in New York City. *Above:* The Recreation Building (as it looked circa 1930) is now known as the Great Hall. It is one of five Greek Revival–style buildings found at Snug Harbor Cultural Center.

Traditional Tranquility

The Staten Island Botanical Garden encompasses several outdoor gardens, including the New York Chinese Scholar's Garden (seen here), which uses ancestral designs that date back nearly 2,000 years. According to tradition, Scholar's Gardens were built for scholars or administrators who had retired from the emperor's court.

Five Victorian houses are currently being used for Snug Harbor's Artist-In-Residence Program. Here, artists and scholars find a quiet place to work and study.

THE ST. GEORGE THEATRE

From its opening on December 4, 1929, to its continued success during the 1940s and beyond, the St. George Theatre hosted celebrities such as Al Jolson, Guy Lombardo, and Kate Smith. During its heyday, movies and vaudeville acts headlined at the 3,000-seat theater, with its gilded balconies, sumptuous grand staircases, and convenient location, just one block from the Staten Island Ferry. Glittering stained-glass chandeliers graced the ceilings; vast murals, tile-decorated fountains, and more adorned the venue.

Eugene De Rosa, the main architect, was assisted by James Whitford, who was known as "the dean of Staten Island architects." The theater's lavish interior was designed by Nestor Castro, who also worked on the interiors of several theaters in the Times Square area.

By 1934, as audience tastes changed, live performances dwindled, but they picked up in the 1940s. Eventually, the venue's focus changed, and it functioned solely as a movie theater until 1972. After that, it was sold several times, unsuccessfully operating as a roller-skating rink, a nightclub, and an antiques showroom. Finally, the theater remained closed for several decades, with just one exception: It was filmed as the backdrop for the big finale in the 2003 Jack Black flick *School of Rock*.

In April 2004, Staten Island dance teacher Rosemary Cappozalo and her daughters took over the theater, transferring ownership to the nonprofit Richmond Dance Ensemble, Inc., which was dedicated to restoring the once opulent theater.

Unfortunately, they found the abandoned venue's plaster walls rife with holes, broken glass, and ripped-out seats. But in the summer of 2004, the St. George Theatre opened once more, wonderfully restored as a 1,800-seat performing arts center. The theater has since presented entertainers including Tony Bennett, *American Idol* winner Taylor Hicks, Art Garfunkel, and the Alvin Ailey American Dance Theater.

Top: The St. George Theatre (shown in 1930) was the brainchild of Solomon Brill, who owned several other theaters in the New York City area. The theater boasted a top-of-the-line Wurlitzer organ and an advanced cooling & heating system (above).
Right: A 1930s-era program from the St. George Theater touts the annual *Jungle and Cartoon Jamboree*. The show featured popular animated characters including Tom & Jerry, Bugs Bunny, and Popeye. Kids could catch the 2½-hour-long show for only 50 cents.

Above: The exterior of the St. George Theatre on Hyatt Street. The theater cost $500,000 to build, which was a huge sum at the time of its opening in 1929. *Left:* The sparkling chandeliers and gilded decorations of the restored St. George Theatre shine once more.

PULLING STRINGS

ENTER THE MANDOLIN BROTHERS SHOWROOM on Forest Avenue and you'll be surrounded by fans of fretted instruments who look as if they've landed in a musical paradise. The store may bill itself as "The Center of the Acoustic Universe," but you only have to travel to Staten Island to experience the showroom *The Boston Globe* dubbed "one of the best guitar shops in the world."

Opened in 1971, the musical emporium has sold and repaired vintage and modern acoustic guitars, twangy banjos, Hawaiian ukuleles, ornamented mandolins, and other stringed instruments. The Staten Island landmark has long lured aspiring musicians and professionals alike, with past visits by luminaries such as George Harrison (the store was shut down to all but the former Beatle to avoid a mob scene), Paul Simon, Judy Collins, and Bob Dylan.

THE STATEN ISLAND FERRY

In the 1600s, the only way to travel from Staten Island to Manhattan was by water, which was often nothing more than a rowboat or sailboat crossing the five miles of harbor between the two islands. By the early 1800s, sloops ferried passengers as well as farm animals and produce. In 1817, New York's first steamboat ferry, the *Nautilus,* began operating between the island and Manhattan. In 1886, Staten Island became easier to reach when a hub was created to link the ferries with railroad service on the island.

In 1905, New York City's Department of Docks and Ferries took over the operations of the Staten Island Ferry and brought in five new vessels, each named for a different borough. Eventually, the fleet was expanded and all the ferries were painted bright orange for greater visibility to other vessels in inclement weather.

In 1897, passengers paid five cents for a one-way trip on the Staten Island Ferry. Over the years, the fare slowly increased; by 1990, a one-way ride had risen to 50 cents. On the Fourth of July, 1997, however, the fare was eliminated altogether—passengers now ride for free on one of NYC's best bargains. The 25-minute ride takes passengers through New York Harbor, with views of Governors Island and the Statue of Liberty.

Each year, approximately 20 million people sail from St. George Terminal on Staten Island to Whitehall Street in Manhattan. On a typical day, five ferries make 100 trips across the harbor, transporting 60,000 passengers between the two boroughs. One of the newest additions to the fleet is the *Spirit of America,* in service since 2005. The ferry's keel was built with steel recovered from the destruction of the World Trade Center on September 11, 2001, and it serves to honor the victims of those attacks.

In this 1917 photo of the ferry *Manhattan,* the lower deck is shown divided into separate cabins for men and women.

Right: A sketch shows the outcome of the disaster on the *Westfield* ferry. On July 30, 1871, the docked ferry's boiler exploded, instantly killing 66 passengers and injuring 200 others. Fifty-nine passengers later died of injuries sustained during the incident.

Below: The unmistakable bright-orange color of the Staten Island Ferry's fleet makes it easy to identify and easy to see, even in dense fog.

THE JACQUES MARCHAIS CENTER OF TIBETAN ART

Despite the name, Jacques Marchais was neither French nor a man. The woman behind the alias, Jacqueline Klauber, grew up in Illinois during the late Victorian era. While searching through her family's attic, she discovered 13 small bronze figurines from Tibet. They had belonged to her great-grandfather, a merchant. The exotic artwork fascinated her, and it eventually led to a lifelong interest in Tibetan culture.

Later in life, she became an art dealer in Manhattan, taking the professional name Jacques Marchais. From the 1920s through the late '40s, she assembled a collection of Tibetan and Himalayan objects. Although Marchais never visited Tibet, she greatly admired the culture and hoped to make people in the West aware of these traditional treasures.

Marchais purchased multicolored *thangkas* (religious Tibetan Buddhist paintings) depicting compassionate deities such as the Green Tara, a goddess, as well as those displaying wrathful images. She bought Buddha statues, ritual artifacts, and musical instruments used in Buddhist ceremonies from Tibet, Mongolia, Nepal, and Northern China. Smiling and frowning dance masks, glittering jewelry, and many-armed statues are included in one of the largest privately owned collections of its kind.

Seeking a permanent home for her collection, Marchais purchased land on Lighthouse Hill on Staten Island, one of the highest points on the Eastern seaboard. On October 5, 1947, the Jacques Marchais Museum of Tibetan Art formally opened to the public. Today, prayer flags flutter in the museum's garden, and a lotus-and-goldfish-filled pond invites quiet meditation. The museum hosts Tibetan Buddhist celebrations, including the creation of mandalas, huge geometric images carefully handcrafted from grains of colored sand. The Dalai Lama, Tibet's religious leader in exile, has visited the museum and has praised the building's authentic appearance.

Above: Art and artifacts fill the library at the Jacques Marchais Museum of Tibetan Art, seen here in 1945. Jacques Marchais assembled a collection of about 1,000 books on Asian art and culture, with an emphasis on Tibetan and Buddhist topics. *Right:* Tibetan Buddhist prayer flags wave in the breeze outside the museum's main building.

HISTORIC RICHMOND TOWN

In the early 1600s, there were only a handful of settlements in the Dutch colony of Staten Island. In 1664, the British took control and the island became known as the County of Richmond. Since the original Richmond Town was centrally located, the local Dutch Reformed congregation chose the village as their religious center in 1695. They built a meetinghouse and residence there for Hendrick Kroesen, their lay minister and teacher, who lived there with his family until 1701.

Around that time, Richmond Town, with its Dutch, English, and French residents, also became the center of Richmond County's government. By the early 19th century, in response to Manhattan's increasingly crowded conditions, some wealthy inlanders flocked to Staten Island's shores and hilly expanses and built serene estates. Richmond Town enjoyed expanded growth; in 1837, its prestige rose with the addition of a courthouse. But when Staten Island became one of New York City's boroughs in 1898, the seat of its government eventually moved to St. George.

But the Staten Island Historical Society hoped to preserve the increasingly fading Richmond Town. In the 1950s, the society reached an agreement with New York City's government and eventually turned the town into an open-air museum. Today, 27 buildings have been restored, including the town's oldest structure, the Britton Cottage, built in 1670. The town bridge, dating from 1845, is Staten Island's only surviving stone arch bridge. Hendrick Kroesen's house also still stands, and it is currently a National Historic Landmark.

Museum employees in period costume demonstrate traditional skills and familiarize visitors with the everyday lives of the town's original residents. Changing exhibits and workshops are scheduled throughout the year, and visitors can enjoy occasional concerts with fiddle and banjo music played against a backdrop of a restored tavern's wood-burning stove and flickering candlelight.

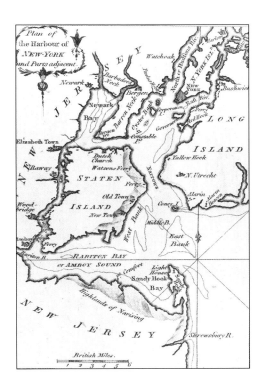

History Comes Alive

At left, an old map of New York harbor shows Staten Island as it looked in the mid-1700s. Historic Richmond Town tries to maintain the feel of the era. The Christopher House (below) is a stone farmhouse that was built circa 1720. The house was the property of Joseph Christopher, who was a member of the county's committee of safety. Although the house was originally in nearby Willowbrook, it was later moved to Historic Richmond Town.

INDEX